D1282593

PEPPER!

Also by Al Thomy

RAMBLIN' WRECK

PEPPER!

The Autobiography of an Unconventional Coach

BY PEPPER RODGERS AND AL THOMY

DOUBLEDAY & COMPANY, INC.
GARDEN CITY, NEW YORK, 1976

RANDALL LIBRARY UNC-W

796.33
R

ISBN: 0-385-11667-5
Library of Congress Catalog Card Number 76-28559
Copyright © 1976 by Pepper Rodgers and Al Thomy
All Rights Reserved
Printed in the United States of America
First edition

c.2

GV
939
.R62
A36

To . . .
The late Franklin Cullen Rodgers, Sr., one of life's most unforgettable characters

and to . . .
Mrs. Blanche M. Thomy, who believes her son should quit following games and settle down to a nice respectable business

Contents

Acknowledgments

For their courtesies and assistance in jogging memory cells, the authors wish to thank Jim Minter of the Atlanta *Constitution;* Tom McEwen of the Tampa *Tribune;* Rex Edmondson of the Jacksonville *Journal;* Jack Hairston of the Gainesville, Florida, *Sun;* Edwin Pope of the Miami *Herald;* Bobby Dodd, Doug Weaver, and Suzanne Blakeney of Georgia Tech; Tommy Prothro of the San Diego Chargers; Terry Donahue of UCLA; John Hunsinger and Sam Lyle; and Doubleday editor Tom Hyman.

PEPPER!

Chapter I   *A Restless Flame on a Honda*

An autumn Saturday dawns over Atlanta and Pepper Rodgers pops awake before 5 A.M. There will be a game at 2 P.M. at Grant Field, and the anticipation makes sleep fitful. Slipping into work clothes and pulling a white helmet over his head, he slips quietly out of the house, cranks up his faithful Honda, and cruises through the deserted streets to the Georgia Tech athletic department. Along the way he pauses for a few minutes at an all-night grocery store where he scans the magazine rack. No use buying any. As a speed reader, he has already devoured the worthwhile articles.

The ritual at his office is the same as always. He changes into sweat clothes and jogs three miles on the oval track around the artificial turf at Grant Field. This physical exertion is more than exercise for him. It puts him in a slower gear, relaxes his restless spirit, and makes the long wait until kickoff more palatable. Following a shower, he jumps on the Honda and it belches down the street to the Silver Skillet, where he wolfs down bacon and eggs. He eats too fast, as if he might miss something. Anything.

Once back at his office, he finds the loneliness wearing and he picks up the phone and calls one of the few people awake at that time of a Saturday morning, Skinny Bobby Harper, a disc jockey at WGST on the Georgia Tech campus.

"Come on over and rap with listeners," Harper says. If Harper had asked the day before, Rodgers probably would have turned him down. He operates on impulse and spontaneity. While most football coaches would recoil in abject horror at a public confrontation before a game, Rodgers welcomes a little mental wrestling.

He craves intellectual and conversational stimulation. Once, when forced to wait for an appointment with a lawyer, he startled those in the reception room by doing push-ups and standing on his head. "It made for good conversation," he says. "I could hear the whispering, 'What's he doing?' and, 'Is he some kind of nut?' and, 'Is he on something?' A farmer, in bib overalls, grabbed his wife and got the hell out of there."

Rodgers does not object to a public press conference the morning before a game because he is a master at logic and the put-down. He has a way with words. Some would call it sophistry.

When a listener with a long memory asks if indeed it was true Rodgers once had a fist fight with a 230-pound linebacker at the University of Florida, he is ready.

"You've got to be out of your ever-lovin' mind," he says.

"At my size, 5-10, 170 pounds, I wouldn't fight a circus midget. I am a lover, not a fighter."

Fans love to zero in on Rodgers. He is vulnerable because he makes positive statements—"Sure, we've got a good team"—and he is visible, not isolated as so many of his coaching colleagues. It is the same with players. He talks with them man-to-man, and he might just say, "We're going to do it my way because I am the coach, dammit." They call him Pepper. "Don't think the players will take the blame (for losses)," he says. "They'll try to blame the coaches, and the coaches will try to blame the players. As head coach, I tell them the responsibility is mine."

He spends two hours at the radio station answering questions of friends and critics, then returns to his office and switches on his elaborate stereo unit. As an unabashed music freak, he leans toward soft rock. He does not have many close friends, but, significantly, one is Phil Walden of Capricorn Records in Macon, Georgia, discoverer of the late Otis Redding and prime mover behind Gregg Allman. Walden sends most Capricorn new releases to Rodgers and occasionally makes a trip with the Georgia Tech football team.

"Listen to this," Rodgers says as he places a cassette into the player. Before the number has ended, he has switched to another. He seldom listens to a complete song.

He says his legacy at UCLA, where he coached before returning to his alma mater, was a juke box in the players' locker room.

"Toughest part about football is getting to the game," he says. "Passing time before the kickoff is physically tiring. Tension is tiring, sapping strength and quickness. Music is diversion. Music that you really don't hear determines your mood. There is music you play when you want to sing, a fight song that picks you up and makes you want to play, a Marine Corps song that makes you feel patriotic."

Rodgers is reminded of a story Bobby Dodd told him about his playing days under General Bob Neyland at Tennessee. Caught in a poker game before a game, Dodd received a lecture from the autocratic Neyland, who insisted on absolute concentration and dedication.

Dodd understood this. He also understood people.

He argued his case.

"Coach Neyland," he said, "I've already got myself completely prepared for the game. I know what I am going to do in every field situation. There is nothing more I can do. Poker relaxes me."

Some coaches confuse being quiet and eating in monastic silence with dedication. Not Rodgers. He prefers noise, music, other diversions.

"Some coaches want you to do what other people told them to do," he says. "Because it was done in the past doesn't make it right."

Anyway, music is Rodgers' thing, and now he is sitting in his office and listening to mood changers as high school prospects arrive and are ushered in for interviews. Blacks are comfortable with the soul background music, and Rodgers, being a sensitive recruiter, does not serenade them with Country and Western. If the conversation is provocative, he lingers with a prospect. If not, the interview is cut short.

"Pepper does not suffer a bore," says close friend Doug Weaver.

Once the recruiting business is done, wife Janet drops in for a brief visit because, after all, she was asleep when Pepper left home.

It is a most unusual scene in a coach's office before a game. They do a little smooching and the music moves Rodgers to dance the bump with his wife.

He grins.

"Wonder if Bear Bryant and John McKay dance the bump before a game?" he says with a mischievous gleam. "I've got 'em all fooled. People think I'm in here drawing X's and O's and worrying about the game. For years coaches have built up this mystique about the game. Their secrecy perpetuates it; otherwise it wouldn't be a mystique."

Dance session ended, Janet Rodgers makes her way to the coach's booth in the press box, and Pepper holds a brief meeting with the team and then trots to the stadium. It is still early, kickoff ninety minutes away, and for him idle time is lost time. He chats with his television show producer, Bob Giordano, and they decide on some pre-game filming in the stands. But first he grabs a hot dog.

Most major college coaches consider Sunday television shows part of the spoils of the profession and an extension of their jobs. For an hour or so spent rehashing game films they receive anywhere from $10,000 to $25,000, and it is easy money needing very little in-put. A play-by-play sheet provided by the college's sports information director is the only script necessary. That is the traditional coach's show, not the Rodgers show. His is more in the Cecil B. DeMille pattern—if not in numbers, then in ideas. He shows very little game action. ("If people want to see the game, they should be at the stadium on Saturday.") He combines a talk show with informal interviews featuring players, trainers, fans, coaches, show business personalities, and politicians. He takes viewers into half-time locker rooms, into the stands, and onto the sidelines to hear coaches coaching live and in living color.

Rodgers has an uncanny way of taking the sting out of criticism. For example, during a long dry spell when his Georgia Tech wasn't doing well and critics were saying he could not win with the run-oriented wishbone offense, he spotlighted five celebrities—Atlanta Falcon coach, Norm Van Brocklin; Atlanta Hawks coach, Cotton Fitzsimmons; actress Dyan Cannon; and presidential candidates Jimmy Carter and Ronald Reagan—all asking the same question:

"Pepper, why don't you pass more?"

The off-beat nature of his show upsets traditionalists, but Rodgers points to his ratings. As a contrast to most film-showing coaches' shows, which attract 3 to 4 per cent of the viewing audience, "The Pepper Rodgers Show" in 1975 drew 48 per cent of the television-viewing audience in Atlanta. Then a strange thing happened. Some of the more conventional coaches started spouting one-liners and changing formats to include human-interest films. Vince Dooley, coach of arch-rival Georgia, permitted cameras in his locker room for his half-time talk, and that was a grudging concession.

Perhaps Rodgers' favorite television story involves Ralph (Shug) Jordan, highly successful and respected head coach at Auburn before his retirement after the 1975 season.

Ten minutes before the Georgia Tech-Auburn game of 1974, Rodgers approached Jordan at midfield.

"Coach, could we shoot an interview for my TV show?" he asked.

"Sure, Pepper, when?"

"Now."

"Now? You mean RIGHT NOW, ten minutes before the game? I don't even talk with my wife ten minutes before a game."

That was against all tradition. No interviews, no frivolous stuff before a serious football game. There was one thing to do before a game. Worry.

Rodgers finally convinced Jordan.

A year later Auburn played at Grant Field and Jordan went looking for Rodgers.

"Hey, Pepper, do you want me to be on your TV show this year?" he asked.

Rodgers was elated.

"After being at Auburn for twenty-five years, he did something different in his life, and he enjoyed it," Rodgers says. "That was good. Who said a football coach must strap himself in like General George Patton and complain his career is in the hands of immature eighteen-year-olds? War is hell, but football is a game."

The story of Rodgers' life is that he has an unreal ability to turn disaster into personal gain, as we shall see in ensuing chapters. He did it as a child, as a collegian, as an assistant coach, a head coach, and on the night of November 27, 1975, he converted a national television tragedy into a public relations coup.

The old guard coaches thought Rodgers a bit off-center when he agreed to let American Broadcasting Company sports producer Chuck Howard station live cameras for the half-time ritual. To coaching conservatives it was blatant heresy. You just don't do those things. Rodgers did.

And probably for a minute or two he wished he had not. He never dreamed he would be exposed to all those people in televisionland trailing arch-rival Georgia, 28–0. What do you say? Go out and win one for Pepper? You've let me down, you've let the school down? If you regulars don't play ball, I'm going to demote the whole crew and play the reserves? Really, what do you say?

Viewers did not know what to expect of the unpredictable Rodgers, but they loved the predicament. It was the stuff most television shows are made of, suffering and public humiliation, the usual script for soap operas or watching the faces of losers on the "Dating Game."

But this was Rodgers' kind of stage, millions watching and his chance to emote as he had done as a three-year-old dancer at the old Loew's Grand in Atlanta.

He began.

"We've seen teams down twenty-eight to zero before," he said. "We're the same team we were before that happened. Maybe we'll come back, maybe we won't. There is a difference in winning and a difference in losing. Winning's all right, losing's all right. We don't know how it will turn out. But there is one request I have of you. Don't quit. That's the worst thing you can do.

"They [Georgia] would like for us to quit. They'd like to rub our noses in the dirt. But I don't want you to let that happen and I know you won't.

"We're not playing for people watching on TV—they've probably given up and turned off their sets by now—or the people in the stands. We are playing for ourselves, you, the coaches, us. We're together and we'll fight. We won't give up. Promise me that. I want you to make Georgia fight for every yard, every first down, play every play like it was your last one."

Rodgers turned to one of his players, Red McDaniel.

"Can we do it, Red?" he asked.

"Yes, sir," said McDaniel, quietly.

"We've fumbled the ball away, we've had a kick blocked, we've been intercepted, what else can we do?" said Rodgers. "We can play the second half. That's what we can do."

With that, Rodgers ended the impassioned plea and the cameras returned to the field. It would be in the Knute Rockne tradition to say Georgia Tech came back and won in the second half. That didn't happen. But the Yellow Jackets scored twenty-six points in the fourth quarter and lost, 42–26, much more respectable than 28–0. They didn't quit and Rodgers received letters from friends and strangers throughout the country supporting his talk.

"That's what I've been trying to tell my boy for years," wrote one Little League father. "You said it so well, and it meant more coming from a coach."

So Pepper Rodgers had taken a setback, a negative happening, and turned it into a gain, a positive situation. That has been the story of his life.

Now, back on game day, Rodgers grabs a microphone and sprints up the stadium steps to laugh and argue with students and take gentle needling about his newspaper quotes. They throw quotes back at him and he loves it. His rapport with young people is much stronger than with older alumni who disapprove of his mod clothes, his shoulder bag, and his motorcycle. Some claim it is a put-on, an obvious attempt to recruit blacks, but Sam Lyle, a former assistant at Georgia Tech, one of Pepper's college coaches, disagrees. "He was always this way, a free spirit, perhaps repressed at times, but a free spirit," he says. "This is the real Pepper Rodgers."

He is uninhibited, true, but Rodgers' pregame energies and actions are misleading.

He had the answer when another coach said Rodgers' actions puzzled him.

"I can't understand why you can be so loose before a game when most coaches and players are in the locker room throwing up," he said.

"That's why I am loose," Rodgers replied. "I don't want to be in the locker room throwing up."

After grandstand interviews, Rodgers retreats to the locker room, has a few words with coaches, and then leads the team on the field for the game. This time he is playing it straight, dressed out in a turned-down sailor's cap and in blue sweater and trousers, running in that awkward little gait of his. There was the time at Kansas in 1967 when he turned cartwheels leading his team on the field and made the national wire services and sports pages. Can anyone imagine Bear Bryant turning cartwheels? Or John McKay? Or Dan Devine? Or Darrell Royal?

It does not bother Rodgers that critics accuse him of gimmickry.

"If they knew me, they'd know that isn't so," he says. "I have always been this way. I do things because they make me feel good. At Kansas I felt like doing a forward roll, and I did it. If someone asked me to do a forward roll, I wouldn't. It has to be spontaneous, something I FEEL like doing. People have a hard time understanding that. I do things off the top of my head.

"When I stood on my head in that lawyer's office, I FELT LIKE doing it. So the word gets around that Rodgers stands on his head and people say, 'Let's go over and watch Rodgers stand on his head.' Doesn't work that way. It is like impressionistic dancing. I do what I feel like doing when I feel like doing it."

As kickoff approaches, Rodgers undergoes a metamorphosis on the sidelines, and the frivolity is gone.

"Funny thing about Pepper," says television producer Giordano who has been on the sidelines with him for two years. "Once the preliminaries end and he goes to work, he quits being the entertainer and becomes the football coach. He is very serious about what he is doing. At times he loses his temper, but only with coaches, not players."

A few minutes after the game starts Rodgers cannot find one of his assistants, Bud Casey.

"Casey, where are you?" he shouts. "Where are you, Casey?"

Casey appears.

Rodgers puts a hand on Casey's shoulder.

"Casey," he says, "the next time I can't find you, then when I find you I am going to kiss you in the mouth right out in front of thousands of fans. It won't hurt me because everyone knows I am crazy. But they're going to think you're gay."

Casey smiles.

Then Rodgers turns to a player and from the stands it appears he is reading the riot act—and he claims he doesn't chew out players on the sidelines.

"That was one of the many heavy decisions I make on the sidelines," he says in explanation. "It was one of the major decisions a coach has to make. The player did something awful. He didn't fumble or miss a pass or mess up a play. He kicked one of the managers in the balls, and I told him if there is one thing we don't do on the sidelines, it's kick managers in the balls. It is not very gentlemanly.

"When the public sees these things from the stands, they don't realize how momentous these decisions are.

"We've had a girl manager at Georgia Tech and I had to discipline her. In requesting a football, she yelled at a player, 'Hey, asshole, throw me a football.' I informed her that, as head football coach, I had the only authority to call anyone an asshole. No others are permitted to use that description. A coach has to have some privileges."

Now it is the fourth quarter and Georgia Tech has fallen behind and Rodgers is pacing the sidelines, yelling instructions and sniping at officials. Then when all hope has been abandoned, he is relaxed and resigned. He has coached as much as he can and there will be another day. He walks behind the bench, sticks his head into the television camera and says, "What a licking!" Then he looks at his watch and says, "It's past my bedtime."

The final gun sounds ending the game, and as he jogs to the locker room Rodgers is met by a drunk.

"Whatcha goin' say now?" the tipsy one says.

For the first time, Rodgers is mad.

"What am I going to say?" he simmers. "I am going to say two of my players suffered broken legs and one might never play again and my players have been working since last September to do the best they can. They're giving it everything they have while guys like you are sitting in the stands drinking your whiskey and complaining about us losing a game. What am I going to say? I am going to say you are to be pitied. You have the problem, not my players."

Rodgers meets with players for a few minutes, then dresses in his fanciest mod clothes, grabs wife Janet by the arm, walks by the opponents' dressing room so they can see him, unlocks the door to his Mercedes and drives off into the night.

Next week he might do something different at a game. Chances are he will.

Pepper Rodgers acts out many roles. In order to coach, he has to be a salesman, selling players on his program. He is a super salesman who regularly lectures to IBM executives in Atlanta on the subject of motivation. Then he is a fun person who needs to be continually stimulated, to do something different in his life. He is a product of whimsey and impulse. Thirdly, he is a football coach who bleeds and hurts.

As he says, "On the outside I do all those things that keep me alive. I enjoy doing what I do at the moment to combat boredom. But after a loss my stomach hurts and my back aches. I hurt all over. I just don't show it."

Rodgers is unpredictable because he detests the predictable. As a Kansas admirer once put it, "Living with Pepper Rodgers is like opening a new box of crackerjacks every morning."

Chapter II   *If I Do Things Differently,*
                 Maybe It's Because I'm Standing
                 on My Head

Actor Tom Laughlin and I had an agreement. I'd put him on the bench for the Rose Bowl game, and he'd find a part for me in a movie. I almost got him there but an unfunny thing happened to my UCLA team on the way to the Rose Bowl. We had to play Southern Cal for that right in the last game of the 1973 season, and instead of advancing to Pasadena, we returned to Westwood with a 24–13 defeat that can be attributed to six turnovers.

Soon thereafter the summons came. Or, as Bear Bryant would have put it, "Mama called." George Mathews, who had been an outstanding football player at Georgia Tech under Bobby Dodd, called to say Bill Fulcher was quitting as head coach and asked if I'd be interested in the job.

I told him I would.

We talked and then I met with him and George Morris in Dallas and there were more discussions. To be honest about it, I had wanted to coach at my alma mater for many years prior to the offer in '73, but until then, the feeling wasn't mutual. I wanted the job when Bud Carson left after the 1971 season, and there were some feelers and contacts, but Frank Broyles was the man Tech wanted, and for whatever reasons—investments or longevity at Arkansas—he didn't want to make the move.

Five years ago I would have walked from Los Angeles to Atlanta for the Georgia Tech job.

"But now you've got to *want* me," I told Mathews.

Our talks bore fruit on the basic issues, and despite rumors to the contrary, they didn't involve a lot of money, my becoming athletic director, easing the entrance requirements, or generally making things easy for me by redesigning Georgia Tech into a football factory. It boiled down to wanting to come to Georgia Tech and being wanted by Georgia Tech. There are cynics who won't believe this, but money never meant that much to me. But Georgia Tech meant that much, and to this day I still get the same thrill of watching the Ramblin' Wreck come out on the field before the game that I got when I sold peanuts in Grant Field as a kid.

Be that as it may, I met later with coach Dodd and Dr. Joseph Pettit, the school president, and took the job. A press conference was scheduled for Tuesday, December 4, 1973, for the announcement.

I didn't make it. But Tom Laughlin called. Even though I had failed in my part of the agreement, and he would never sit on my UCLA bench in the Rose Bowl, he called to say he had a part for me in his movie, *The Trial of Billy Jack.*

He said, "Pepper, you gonna be the baddest dude that ever walked."

And, was I bad! I jetted to Arizona to shoot my movie part in one day—$138 base pay and $3 meal money—and I was plenty bad.

I play an onery state trooper, and I and some other troopers capture Billy Jack and try to get him to make a break for it so we can gun him down. I shoot him, but he gets away. That's a bad dude.

Finally, Billy Jack steals one of our cars and he's going to run us down. Before we shoot the scene, Tom looks over to me. "Pepper," he says, "you're not going to get me on the bench for that Rose Bowl game so you better be agile when I start this car."

Shooting the scene was fun. I loved it. And, Georgia Tech job or no job, I wasn't going to pass up this opportunity to do what I always wanted to do, act in a movie. So, on Wednesday, a day late, without a minute's sleep, I walk into the Georgia Tech athletic building to become the sixth head coach in the school's history. The kid who sold peanuts in Grant Field, the Boy Scout who ushered in the West Stands, the quarterback who played on some of Bobby Dodd's greatest teams had returned as the head coach.

I wasn't prepared for the first question.

"Why would you leave a successful football program at UCLA to come back to Georgia Tech where the football fortunes have been on decline?" a reporter asked.

I didn't need any reason to come back to my home

town and my alma mater. If it had been Northwestern or
SMU, I wouldn't have left UCLA. But to return to Georgia Tech I needed no reason. It was probably the only
school for which I would have left UCLA, which certainly has one of the finest athletic programs in the country.

I don't claim to be a miracle coach, as I didn't claim to
be a miracle player. For a guy who started only six games
in three years at Georgia Tech, I received maximum exposure. And for a coach with my record, fluctuating around
the .500 mark, I think I am the best-known coach in the
country. As a player I knew what I could do. I could
place-kick and I could pass. I never made myself look bad
by trying to do something else. I did what I could do. As
a coach I know what I can do.

"Do you think you can win at Georgia Tech?" a reporter asked me.

And I said, "No, I came here to lose."

I have been called an iconoclast because I don't do the
things other coaches do off the field. If I feel like turning
a cartwheel before a game, I do it. If I feel like putting on
a wig and singing a rock song for my team, I do it. If I
feel like riding a motorcycle to work, I do it. If I don't
feel like wearing a coat and tie, I don't. If I believe the
game of football should be fun, I try to make it fun. If
that makes me an iconoclast, a wrecker of traditions, then
I am an iconoclast. But I don't think it does. I believe in
tradition, but I don't believe you should do something
just because someone else did it. You should do it if that
is the best thing to do. I do the things that keep me alive.

Football is not World War III. It is a game, and I try to remember that.

If I had my choice, I'd play football as they play rugby —at the end of a rugby game everyone comes out to the middle of the field, pops a keg, and sits around and drinks beer and sings songs. They don't need state troopers to protect coaches nor do they worry about some nut running out from the stands and punching them in the nose. Rugby players and fans mingle together after a match, and they enjoy the sport for what it is—a sport.

At the risk of offending purists, I must say we in football are in danger of taking ourselves too seriously. The recent strike in professional football was an example. Players have to figure out what they are worth and how far they can go. Obviously, plumbers can go a lot farther than football players. We do not need football—I know where I stand—but we sure as hell need plumbers because the public becomes concerned when there is no water. Football is a luxury. Once the mystique wears off and the superstar is seen carrying a picket sign the public asks, "What are you giving me for my money?"

There is no mystique to football. It is a boy's game played by the man-boy. The game has no problem. Those who make a holy crusade out of it, do.

I like the story that Bill Curry, our offensive line coach, tells about his days with the Green Bay Packers. They were discussing the Ten Commandments when the team trainer said the thirteenth commandment was the most important.

"The thirteenth?" said Curry. "What is that?"

"It's this," said the trainer. "'Don't take yourself too seriously.'"

As an example of those who would make football a crusade, I cite another Southern tradition we no longer have at Georgia Tech, the football game invocation.

There was a lot of flak about the abolition of the pregame prayer.

Why for goodness sake? I tell them that Dr. Pettit is the invocation coach. No matter what you say about invocations and prayer, you're wrong. If you say it has no place at a football game, you make everyone mad. If you say you should have an invocation, then you get mired in denominationalism. It is not my responsibility to actively pursue the way I feel, whether religious, ethnic or political. I'm not going to try and convert every Jew or Moslem to Christianity. As old-fashioned as it may seem, I think the Golden Rule is the best guide; treat others as you would want them to treat you. You can dislike someone for what he does to you at a specific time, but don't dislike him because he is what he is—black, white, Catholic, Protestant, or Jew.

During a recent banquet I turned to a neighbor and asked him, "Why do you say grace here when you don't say grace at home?" It didn't make sense.

I have people call and ask me to speak at their church and they mention "image." I ask them why. Is it because I am divorced and remarried? Because I carry a shoulder bag? Because I sign "too many black players?" Because I don't wear a coat and tie all the time? Then they tell me to bring Lucius Sanford, one of our black players. That's a concession. I tell them I can't make it, I'm going to

Martin Luther King's church. I have been there. It's the kind of experience I like, a good feeling. I guess I'm a pollyanna at heart. Do you know how many people want to see the bad in you? Thousands. Do you know how many people want to see the good in you? Very few. When my coaches mention a high school prospect I always tell them I want to hear something good about him before they tell me the bad. Even if it's only that his mother and father are good. And when we diagram a play on the blackboard I want somebody to say something good about it before we criticize it. If you rip it apart, no one will put a play on the board.

If you cut me up, you'd see a religious person inside, in my way of being religious. I might not be religious in a church-going way. I don't go to a church; I go to see or hear a preacher. I don't think I have to justify my existence as a coach by saying in my biography that I'm a deacon in the church. Some of the worst coaches I know have that on their resumé. They talk about me and they talk about other people.

Recruiting can be the nastiest business of all. We had a problem with recruitment of Mackel Harris, a great prospect from Americus, Georgia, because a recruiter from another school told his mother, and I quote directly, "In Atlanta they hold boys down and shoot dope into their veins." She cried when he decided to come to Georgia Tech. That's the part of recruiting I don't like. And those recruiters probably say they're religious.

After a game during the season, a prominent alumnus of Georgia said, "God was with Georgia today."

The next week when we played in Atlanta I wondered

if God came from Jacksonville for the game. The point is this: I think God didn't mean for football to be the main issue on a Saturday afternoon. He has more important things to do than be at the Georgia Tech-Georgia game. Invocations are strictly a Southern tradition. We didn't have them on the West Coast and I don't think Notre Dame has them. That doesn't mean we Southerners are hung up on traditions. But we are more traditional and even more law-abiding because once a law is on the books, that's it. After coming back to Tech, I attended a football banquet at Griffin, Georgia, and it was a warm affair, whites and blacks mingling in harmony, and I'm sure they were being bused. It was a sharp contrast to what happened at Boston.

I just don't think football should be that serious, a culture within a culture.

A couple of years ago when the Georgia Bulldogs opened a week before we did, I packed a picnic lunch and drove over to Athens for a tailgate party and a leisurely afternoon in the sun. I noticed this guy eyeing me from across the aisle, and at half time he came over with his little girl in his arms. She was hardly walking age.

"Honey, this is Coach Rodgers of Georgia Tech," he said.

Then this little doll contorts her face into an ugly mask and in a tiny voice filled with venom shouts, "Dog meat!"

I want to cry.

But instead I say, "Gee, you're mighty sweet to be saying something like that."

You can't blame the little girl. Her father put her up to

it. Still it was sad, not at all what football should be. I try to recruit the Georgia players and Georgia coach, Vince Dooley, tries to recruit the Tech players. I try to beat him and he tries to beat me, but we shouldn't be mortal enemies.

Players also are prone to think football is something it isn't. We were recruiting this high school player from North Carolina when one of our assistants told me we had a problem.

"He says he will come and he is interested in Georgia Tech, er, but, er, but . . ." said one of our coaches.

"But what?"

"But . . . he wants a girl. He says to have a girl available for him."

I blew my top. I told our coach to inform our young friend from the Carolinas we were not running an escort service, and we were interested in him as a student and a football player, not as a playboy or a stud at large. On further thought, I told him to forget it. If that is what it took to bring this boy to school, we did not need him.

No telling how many schools he visited before he made up his mind, this Don Juan of the jock set.

I run a loose ship, but not that loose.

I don't believe in a lot of rules. A coach has much better discipline and morale when he's not on the players' tails all the time. That is the reason I don't adhere to those who advocate athletic dorms. Under that system players form cliques and gripe about coaches. They get weary of each other and can't wait for the chance for break out. And players in athletic dorms do the same things, or more, that other players do. At Kansas we had fights, marijuana, girls in rooms, snakes in rooms, brawls and noise, everything that happens outside of athletic dorms. No matter where the players are, there is no way to watch them all the time. Don't press down on them, and players grow up. Ban something, and that's what they want.

The same applies to dress and grooming codes.

The modern player wears his hair long, prefers mod clothes, and insists on knowing why. There is little difference between the player of today and the player of twenty years ago. We from that era tend to forget our own indiscretions.

My eyes were opened at Kansas when in the midst of a struggling season I confronted one of our defensive ends, Steve Carmichael.

"Don't you think your hair is a little too long?" I said to him.

He gave me a soulful look.

"Coach," he said, "if we were winning I could get a date. But since we're not, it's pretty hard for a guy with a crew cut to get a date."

I understood. It was not a matter of rebellion; it was a matter of style. When I was a student at Georgia Tech, coach Dodd never told me I had to wear my hair long. That's because the style was short, a crew cut. During those days we all peroxided our hair and hitchhiked to Daytona during the spring holidays. No one thought about hair. Then all of a sudden, we start to worry about hair. It doesn't make sense.

A lot of black players wear mustaches, and this bothers some coaches. But blacks have always worn mustaches. Once you quit worrying about it, you don't even notice. I couldn't tell you which of my players have mustaches and which don't. I couldn't tell you what makes them different except for their personalities. I say the athlete of today is better, and I say that with the realization that I don't know what they do in their spare time. I know what I and my friends did in college, and it is not what we'd always like to remember. We had fights and beer parties and carrying on. The only thing that has really changed is our memory.

It is true an athlete has a responsibility, but you cannot shut off a man from life and isolate him because he is an athlete.

About pot and girls and the rest, I don't stick my head in the sand, and I don't want the players to think I don't know what is going on. But these are universal social conditions and not peculiar to football players.

We ask that they go to class and we keep files to check their attendance. If they get in trouble, they are judged just like any other student depending on the severity of the problem. First offenders are judged differently from habitual rule breakers.

What I am saying is that I can't follow athletes around twenty-four hours a day, and those who say they can are speaking out of the sides of their mouths.

Also, I can't coach fifty football players. I coach the coaches and they coach the players. Assistants are extensions of the head coach, and players are extensions of the assistants. If I appear frivolous and loose off the field, I am dead serious when I am coaching. Football is fun before and after practice and during games; practice is not fun. As a player I never cared for practice. But it is there and you make the best of it.

My job is to coach and sell the football program at Georgia Tech, and to do that I'd tap dance, do somersaults leading the team on the field and play tennis with Stan Smith at Five Points in downtown Atlanta. At Georgia Tech we've even utilized an advertising campaign, and that broke a few traditions. College football just doesn't do that.

We have bumper stickers reading, "Pepper Power" emblazoned on a chicken wishbone, symbolizing our wishbone offense. The first year we ran little ads reading, "Pepper's Spicing Things Up," and the next we had them with, "Pepper's Put The Sting Back In" (the Yellow Jackets). The response has been favorable.

Since Georgia Tech had fallen on lean years after being one of the nation's collegiate powers, I didn't feel I could sell Tech football. So I am selling myself, Pepper Rodgers. Go to Georgia Tech and play football for Pepper Rodgers. There has been some criticism. Some say I am concentrating everything into one person, me, but that was the object. Before I came back to Tech, the critics were blaming Dr. Pettit, they were blaming Bobby Dodd, they were blaming the athletic board, and they were blaming the school itself.

Now they can concentrate their blame into me. And that's good. That's the way it should be.

One problem in returning to your old school is that some people expect you to be the same person who left as a student. As I told George Mathews when I accepted the job, "Don't expect the same Pepper Rodgers to step right into character." And when I left school I told coach Dodd I wanted to coach, but I wouldn't be another Bobby Dodd. I'd be Pepper Rodgers.

A man called recently and told me a Georgia Tech coach had spoken at his club for the past twenty years and he expected me to show up.

I told him to ask me and I'd give him an answer.

I don't have to do anything just because it has been done in the past. There are only two things I have to do at Georgia Tech. I have to coach football and I have to win, and I do understand that. Other than that, I have options.

There were some who criticized my life-style, the motorcycle, carrying a shoulder bag, my sailor's cap worn during games. As for the motorcycle, it is something I enjoy. I also have a Cadillac, a Mercedes, an Oldsmobile, and I enjoy those too. The bag is useful to carry my phone book, wallet, and other things in since I wear informal clothes without pockets. If I carried an Adidas bag or a Pan-Am bag, no one would say anything. But a shoulder bag, that's different. The cap serves two purposes. It protects my face, which was badly burned in a boat explosion, and it keeps the sun from oxidizing the hair-coloring and turning my hair red. Now, how's that for honesty?

There has been another change in my life. I was divorced from my first wife, Judy, and remarried.

Judy and I were married during my college days, and we had two kids by the time I graduated. I don't know what happened, but we drifted apart, and I just don't believe in staying together when things aren't right. No one wants to get divorced, but sometimes it is the only course. These things happen. I feel fortunate that in Janet I have a wife, a lover, and a friend, and I don't think many people find that. I keep pretty much to myself in regard to close friendships. I really don't have but two or three. Since I've got a wife, a lover and a friend, all I need is someone else to talk to. What else do you need?

In the past some said I was a vagabond, running in and preaching a little sermon and running out, and I'll admit there was excitement in my life in going from the Air Force Academy to Florida to UCLA to Kansas, back to UCLA, and then to Georgia Tech, not worrying about old places and faces and meeting new people. I don't do that now because I am comfortable with myself. I am happy.

People's lives change.

Still, I am aware there is no way I am going to please everyone, and I understand that.

That reminds me of my favorite story, a parable, if you will.

This lady seeks out a marriage counselor and requests ways of repairing marital fences with her husband who is antagonistic and disagreeable, not to mention mule-headed.

"Be domestic, be agreeable, pamper him," advises the the counselor.

She begins her campaign the next morning.

"Dear, what would like for breakfast?" she asks.

"Two eggs," he says.

"How?"

"One fried and one scrambled."

She sings cheerfully and does his bidding.

Then she places the eggs before him, one scrambled and one fried.

"How's that, dear?" she asks.

He looks at one and then the other.

"Just as I thought," he says, "you fried the wrong damn egg."

The moral of this story: You can't please everybody all of the time, or, no matter what you do, you can't ever please some people.

A coach lives and is on trial from week to week. You win, you're a hero. You lose, you're a bum. If there is one thing that upsets me, it is the guilt feeling forced upon you when you lose. As far as I know you're the same guy you were before the game, but all of a sudden you're a leper, an untouchable. You let down the coaches, the coaches' wives, the players, the alumni, and even the secretaries and the people in the athletic department. When you walk in on a Monday after a Saturday loss, it is like there has been a death in the family. Did your mother die? Did your son die?

The alumni are rebellious. It is as though we don't hurt or bleed, we don't feel. I am sensitive, and most coaches I know are sensitive. We don't like to lose. But losing is a reality of life.

Fans are prone to pinpoint the blame. At Tech in the

opening game of 1975 we lost to South Carolina and the critics blamed the wishbone offense. They said it was not a catch-up offense. My reply was that I did not have a play, wishbone or otherwise, that could carry me eighty yards in sixty seconds. I recalled the Super Bowl of a few years ago and Fran Tarkenton running a pro offense, and he could not catch up with Pittsburgh simply because Mean Joe Greene of the Steelers was beating the hell out of his offensive guard. I haven't seen an offense or any play work when a defensive tackle is tattooing your offensive lineman.

Chapter III   Styes, High-top Shoes, and a Dandy of the Living Stage

If I weren't coaching football, I might be dancing on a television variety show. I could have been a tap dancer. Or a vocalist. But not a clarinetist.

At the age of three I was taking dancing lessons because my mother, who worked every day of her life for more than forty years, thought I should. She had trouble with her vision so I wore glasses I didn't need. When her feet hurt, I wore high top shoes. I grew up with styes, boils on my head, flat feet, pink eyes, anything you can imagine. I consider myself a person who had an inferiority complex and outgrew it. Scholastically, I moved right along after my mother convinced the principal I was so bright there was no use in my loitering in the third grade. I was allowed to skip it.

I don't know why or how but as a kid I began to say positive things that irritated people, and somewhere along the line I began to believe and do the things I talked about. As one who spent a great deal of solitary hours and looked inwardly, I was unflappable when the conversation was in my ballpark. My confidence was fortified by my own preparation.

From ages three to five, my cousin June Ann Rodgers, my pal Buddy Young, and I danced in the Kiddie Review, the biggest thing in Atlanta during those post-depression days, the biggest thing before *Gone with The Wind.* The Kiddie Review was held regularly at Lowe's Grand Theater.

In the modern vernacular, I was a real dude, all dressed up in a tuxedo, walking cane in hand, tap dancing and singing, "I'm a Ding Dong Daddy From Dumas . . . you oughta see me do my stuff." Then I laid 'em in the aisles with "Yankee Doodle Dandy." If nothing else, this gave me stage presence for later in life when I would become a football coach, a profession that includes a great deal of public speaking and public relating.

The stage show business got old, and I retired at the age of six to become the next great clarinet player in the South. There was a slight problem. No aptitude.

People talk about pressure. They say I was under a lot of pressure when I was kicking field goals for Georgia Tech. That is not true. I made field goals because I was good at kicking field goals and at concentrating. All my life I've been able to listen to music without hearing it, look at people without seeing them, blocking out anything I wanted to. That's why I was good at kicking field goals. Now, for real pressure. When I was moved from third to first clarinetist and was asked to play a solo, that was real pressure because I was asked to do something I couldn't do well.

I'll never forget the evening of my first solo. The band director quieted the rest of the band and pointed at me. Nothing came out, not a sound. I froze. My career as a clarinetist was short-lived.

Although not a privileged family, we always had enough to eat. In those days my father, Franklin, wheeled and dealed, buying items cheap and making a profit on them. He also sold insurance, but, mainly, he hung around the politicians at city hall. My mother's steady work meant there was always food in my lunch sack, if nothing but deviled egg sandwiches. For what seemed a year I took three deviled egg sandwiches to school until I got sick of them and plastered the side of the school building with deviled egg. I think it was twenty years before I ate another deviled egg sandwich.

During those formative years my most enjoyable hours were spent at the farm of my grandfather, J. B. Upshaw, a great baseball fan and an incorrigible Civil War buff who entertained my brother Allen and me with tales of Ty Cobb, Walter Johnson and Jeb Stuart, not necessarily in that order. Many was the hour I spent in the backyard sliding into a tow sack and fantasizing I was Ty Cobb the "Georgia Peach." On more serious days I'd be Jeb Stuart riding a white horse and fighting the Yankees. To this day I think Jeb Stuart was a sensational person and I never really knew much about him. I was always someone else, not Pepper Rodgers. That I was a loner probably can be attributed to the fact we moved a lot. And being alone, I read a lot—everything I could get my hands on.

As all families, we had pets. One, a rooster, I didn't particularly care for. He was a terrible-tempered creature and he'd come flapping at me when I invaded his domain. I don't think he was really that vicious, but we'd built him up to be a killer and all of us were afraid of him except my mother, and she wasn't afraid of anything.

Our pride and joy was a pony, Tony the Pony. He was a timid sort that didn't like to stay home so we removed the backseat of the car and chauffeured him around with us, his head sticking out of a back window. I remember one old man saying, "My God, the Rodgerses have the ugliest looking dog in town." But I liked Tony a lot better than I did that damned rooster who was about as big as I was.

Sports were a big item in my life, a way to lose myself in competition.

Our Boy Scout group, Troop 22, had leagues for all sports and we were allowed to usher and sell peanuts at Grant Field where Georgia Tech played home football games. Of all the trips to Grant Field, the 1942 Tech-Georgia game sticks out in my mind. They were playing to see who would go to the Rose Bowl and Tech lost, much to my dismay. I was so emotionally involved that later that evening I picked up the phone and called Clint Castleberry, Tech's big star, to offer condolences. His mother said he wasn't home but she'd deliver the message. Later Castleberry returned my call and I relayed my sentiments. Many call him Tech's greatest player although he played only one year as a freshman before he was inducted into service. He died in a plane crash.

After my days at Joe Brown Junior High I moved on to one of the three high schools, Boys High, as a freshman. Because I was so small and the Boys High football players were so large and so tough looking, I passed up football for another shot at the clarinet, which was another mistake.

I've often thought how little it takes to please a young student. However successful I have been since, I recall that basketball coach Joel Eaves, now athletic director at the University of Georgia, presented me with a little trophy for intramural basketball excellence at Boys High and that stands out in my mind. It probably cost only a few cents, but it meant a great deal to a kid, and I'll always admire coach Eaves for that.

I never would have made it at Boys High. But, fortunately for me, in 1946–47, Atlanta's four high schools—Boys, Tech, Girls, and Commercial—were abolished and the neighborhood system instituted at the seven junior high schools, Bass, O'Keefe, Grady, Smith, Roosevelt, Murphy, and Brown, and I was back in familiar surroundings. For the next three years, with J. E. DeVaughn coaching football and Roy Rowlett basketball, Brown was to dominate city athletics.

I started off in a flurry of stardom in organized athletics, a split end-wingback on the B team, or reserves. But all was not lost. Brown won the city championship and earned a trip to Miami to play Senior High, and as cannon fodder on the B-team, impersonating rival quarterbacks, I was invited along as excess baggage—my reward for being knocked around by the varsity. Little did

Pepper Rodgers know that in Miami he was to receive his first athletic-connected injury.

It occurred not on the field of friendly strife, but on the roof of a Miami Beach hotel.

Someone discovered some naked ladies sunbathing behind a canvas partition and Rodgers, being the clever little quarterback he was, devised an ingenious scheme to get a closer and better look at said objects, namely, taking a razor blade and slitting the canvas. The blade obtained, I tiptoed to the canvas, slit the hole and placed my eye to the canvas. Instead of naked ladies, I saw stars. It seems one of the ladies spotted my shadow, whopped me with her purse, and sent me sprawling across the roof. When I returned to Atlanta with a black eye, friends assumed it was from football practice and I never told them otherwise.

Perhaps it was good I didn't play in the game. Miami Senior High, with such great players as Jim Dooley, Dick Peppler and Bobby Moorhead, gave us a real licking, 48–0. Moorhead later was an all-America defensive back at Georgia Tech.

The next year, with such outstanding talent as Johnny Hunsinger, Charlie Brannon, Bulldog Carithers, Cecil Trainer, Pig Campbell, Don Cox, and Wayne Clyburn around coach DeVaughn went to the T-formation and Brown High was off and running on a high school dynasty, not to mention another city championship.

Somehow, I had to become a part of this success story.

There was only one position I could play, quarterback. But Brown had a talented quarterback in Charlie Brannon. But—Brannon could play any position. Therefore, I settled on a plan based on a precedent. In the ninth grade Hunsinger was the passer and I was the catcher and I had convinced John there was more glory in catching than in throwing and he had become a really fine halfback.

So I went to coach DeVaughn.

I pleaded my case. Sure, Charlie Brannon was a fine quarterback, but he could play other positions. And if he played another position then I could play quarterback and that would be our strongest lineup. That way I could play and Charlie would be no less valuable.

It worked.

As a junior and senior, I was the quarterback and each year we won the city championship. I was not a bad runner. I just looked funny running. And my passing might not have been the prettiest in the world but I seldom missed my receivers. If you can't throw those bullets, then you must fool the defense.

Thinking is what quarterbacking is all about. I worked on it, I studied until late in the night on what I would do in every field situation. I thought I knew about everything that could happen on a football field. But, in 1949, I ran into something entirely foreign to me.

Since we didn't have a plan for it, I improvised.

We had gone to Charlotte, North Carolina, to play a strong Central High School team that featured a couple of outstanding players in Larry Parker and Walter Propst, and Central sprang a new defensive alignment on us, an eight-man line. We had never worked on it before because we had never faced it.

We had a few audibles.

I'd call out something like, "Six-man line, Charlie." That meant that our center, Charlie, would come out of the line to block on the end.

But the eight-man line was something else. The first time Central used it I called out, "Eight-man line, do anything you want to." We had a lot of confusion on the play. Then we went up to the line again and, son of a gun, another eight-man line.

So I called the first scrimmage line audible in Georgia high school history, as far as I know. I said, "Eight-man line, everybody stay and block except Cecil . . . Hike!" Everyone stayed and blocked and I threw a pass to Cecil Trainer for a long gainer.

That year we upset Glynn Academy of Brunswick, Georgia, 37–0, for the state championship and they had one of their finest teams with such great athletes as Bill Brigman, Sonny George, and Bob Sherman tearing up people. They had run over Lanier of Macon by something like 50–0, out of sight.

As a basketball player I led the city in scoring. There was a reason. To Roy Rowlett's distress, I shot more than any other player.

I drove him to distraction.

Once, when another high scorer was hurt, I approached a reporter and said, "Why don't you ask me how we'll adjust to the loss of my teammate?"

He went along.

"Okay," he said, "how will you adjust to the loss?"

"I guess I'll have to shoot more," I said.

The reporter printed the quote and coach Rowlett grew more gray hairs.

Even before Pete Maravich, I had trouble keeping my socks up. And that bothered me. I wanted to look cool like the other guys, but my legs sweated a lot and the damned socks kept slipping. Finally, in disgust, I gave up and let them droop. No matter how I tried I just couldn't look cool.

In those days athletes played all sports, and I did a little infielding on the baseball team. We sort of bombed out in the city championship game, though, losing 10–9 to Marist after leading 9–0 in the second inning. I really feel old when I recall the Marist hero that afternoon was Chappell Rhino, whose two sons played for me at Georgia Tech.

Whatever the sport, cocky little Pepper Rodgers always had an answer.

In one of our baseball games this catcher on the other team was giving me a hard time.

"The great Pepper Rodgers," he said as I came up to bat. "You know what people are saying about you? They're saying you're conceited, that's what they're saying."

That was it, the final straw. I'd had enough.

"And do you know what they're saying about you?" I said.

He took the bait.

"No, what are they saying?"

"Nothing."

I got no more lip from him.

Then came the end of school days at Brown High School and the isolated feeling that colleges were interested in almost all of our players except me. There were scouts all over the neighborhood and when I saw Ray Graves, Georgia Tech defensive coach, I knew something was up. From what I understood, he was stopping off at the homes of Hunsinger, Brannon, Campbell, and Carithers.

Once more Rodgers had to sell himself.

When Graves paused at a neighboring house, I jumped into his car. As we rode from home to home I cited statistics from every game during my career. Then I refused to get out of the car unless I received a Tech scholarship.

Graves, who later was to figure prominently in my coaching career, was exasperated.

"Pepper, if you'll leave me alone, I'll get you a city scholarship for one year," he said.

"That's okay with me," I said. "At the end of my freshman year at Georgia Tech I will have a full scholarship—"

I did.

Chapter IV   *A Snap and a Kick to be a Hero,*
                 a Struggle to Remain One

It was the evening of December 31, 1951, and I relaxed at a Miami beach hotel with my Georgia Tech roommate, Larry Morris, later to be an NFL linebacker of all-Pro caliber. There was no reason to believe I would be a hero the next afternoon in our Orange Bowl game against the Baylor Bears and their great quarterback, Larry Isbell.

I was quite familiar with Isbell. In practices leading up to the bowl game, I WAS Larry Isbell. I impersonated him, his passing, his idiosyncrasies, his demeanor. Which was quite a chore since my passes were more like dying swans and his like lift-offs from Cape Kennedy. There are some who play with the grace of a ballet dancer. Then there are the Pepper Rodgerses, scrambling, manipulating, doing anything to get the job done. But I knew what I could do, and I had supreme confidence in my ability to do it.

Up to that Orange Bowl game, my career at Georgia Tech had been most undistinguished. I appeared on The Flats, as the school is called, in 1950 at a time when

Bobby Dodd's coaching fortunes were at their lowest ebb. Only a victory over arch-rival Georgia prevented that season from being a complete disaster, and even at that, the Jackets had a losing record, 5-6. Fortunately, however, Dodd had had a fruitful recruiting year and Tech was on the verge of its golden modern years, coinciding with the legalizing of two-platoon football. A hint of the future came in the annual Thanksgiving Day freshman classic when we beat Georgia, 54–6. I played three minutes and threw a touchdown pass.

The varsity quarterback at that time was Darrell Crawford and, during my sophomore year, in 1951, I figured I had a chance to play behind him. But a young prospect out of Brunswick, Georgia, Bill Brigman, proved more adroit at handling the belly series installed by coach Dodd, and he relegated me to the third string. To mollify my ego, I always said it was because he was dating coach Dodd's daughter, Linda, but I knew that wasn't true. He had more innate talent.

So, here I was in Miami, hanging on the coattails of the regulars, impersonating the enemy quarterback, or as they say, "a member of the traveling squad."

On that night before the game, I turned to Larry Morris and said, "Larry, I'm going to bed because I have a feeling I will have to kick a field goal to beat Baylor."

He laughed. If I had been in his place, I too would have laughed at such brashness.

Then came the game and I saw more action than I had anticipated. Coach Dodd called on me to kick extra points, and it was 14–14 going into the final minutes.

Things did not look encouraging for us. Then Pete Ferris intercepted Isbell, had clear sailing for the goal, but was overtaken at the Baylor 15. Leon Hardeman nibbled at the huge Baylor line for seven yards in two carries, a Crawford pass fell incomplete, and there we were, fourth-and-three at the Baylor eight.

This was the stage for Pepper Rodgers. The world was watching.

Sam Lyle, one of our assistant coaches, later told me this moment was one of the few times he had seen coach Dodd excited on the sidelines. With the game almost over, he had to be sure.

"Who can kick a field goal?" coach Dodd shouted.

Three hands went up.

He pointed at me.

"Pepper, get in there."

This was my moment. I dashed into the game, surveyed the position, eight-yard line, difficult angle, and I had a suggestion in the huddle.

"Why don't we take a five-yard penalty so I can get a better angle?" I offered.

George Morris, one of the truly great centers and linebackers ever to play the game, looked at me like I was touched in the head.

"We're not taking any penalty, kick the damn ball!" he insisted in a most convincing voice.

I kicked the ball.

I only got nervous when the ball was coming back from center, especially with those gigantic Baylor linemen bearing down on me, but the moment I put my foot into it, I knew it was good and I threw up both hands to signal my success. So, in looking back, I guess I was the first mod player since almost all of them go through strange gyrations after scoring these days.

I was not at all reluctant to play the hero's role after the game. When the Orange Bowl queen and her entourage strolled by at the post-game party looking for the big names, I nominated myself.

"I'm as big a hero as anyone," I told her. She was somewhat dubious because of my size and waterboy appearance, but she joined my table.

A writer asked if I anticipated having such an afternoon, and I laid it on thick.

"Heck, naw," I said. All week I had been telling coach Dodd I ought to practice kicking a lot because I was going to be his hero. The pressure, all this, it was right down my alley.

Sometimes it's hard for a hero to break in.

I kept telling coach Dodd I'd be his hero and he kept smiling. But he wasn't smiling one afternoon during field goal practice when I shanked half of my attempts.

"Don't worry, coach Dodd," I told him. "I'm not hitting them in this empty stadium, but you put fifty thousand people in those seats and ole Pepper won't miss."

Coach Dodd liked that kind of confidence.

Still, I didn't start off on the right foot in my first chance to play quarterback during my sophomore year. When Darrell Crawford got hurt in the Auburn game, I got the call. My first live action was shaky. I fumbled the snap from center, Auburn recovered and Rodgers was back on the bench.

When Crawford went back into the game, I took his place at the phone from the press box where Frank Broyles was charting the game. The next sound I heard was not very pleasant.

"Get that goddam Rodgers out of there!"

I tapped coach Dodd on the shoulder.

"Coach," I said, "I think this call is for you."

I did not approach heroic stature on that afternoon. But with one swipe of my right foot, I made it in the Orange Bowl, and I loved what Colonel Ed Danforth, Atlanta *Journal* sports editor, wrote about my post-kick comportment:

"That gesture, impudent and confident, of raising his arms to indicate a score endeared the boy to one observer. Football players are so disciplined they rarely do anything impulsively beyond cracking an opposing player on the snout in a moment of anger. Tommy Lewis' charge from the bench to tackle a runner and Rodgers' signal were suddenly whimsical moves that lifted them out of the herd."

Perhaps those are the characteristics of my life—impulsive, whimsical, confidence, not a slave to rigidity.

If I was intoxicated by the heady wines of success in January, I was returned to the sobering reality of the world in September.

Old Pepper Rodgers, the hero, the toast of the Orange Bowl, Frank Merriwell, the guy coach Dodd kissed on the forehead on the front pages of all the newspapers, reported for fall practice and found a red shirt in his locker. That was the message I had been demoted to the junior varsity, the scrubs, the reserves. How the hero had fallen!

You want to know what humiliation is?

It is Pepper Rodgers, star of the Orange Bowl game and toast of Atlanta in January, taking that three-block walk from the Tech dressing quarters in Grant Field to our practice area in a red shirt. That was the longest walk of my life, and I felt every eye on campus following me. Although I was never one of coach Broyles' favorites, I fully expected to be the first-string quarterback.

I would be the last to describe myself as a picture-book quarterback. Colonel Danforth put it best when he wrote: "Pepper is precise only when he kicks extra points and field goals. Otherwise, he plays strictly by ear. He is an artist, a master of improvisation. He can call a forward pass deep to the right end and modulate clean through the scale until he whips it to a stray halfback who thought the play was over. It was botched from the start, but it clicks for a touchdown. That's Pepper's way of doing business."

My style was not one to inspire tranquility among the coaches, but I knew what I could do—throw and place-kick—and I did what I had confidence in. Demotion only intensified my determination to play, and after ten days of carrying dummies and bags around, I walked up to coach Dodd.

"Coach, can I tell you something?" I said.

He said, "Sure, Pepper, go ahead."

You could always talk to coach Dodd and he would listen. He liked people with confidence and I knew that.

"Coach Dodd, you know I am too good to be on the Jayvee team," I said.

He looked at me for a moment.

"You're right, I'll take the responsibility," he said.

That might have been a little brazen, but I've always thought you had to fight for something if you wanted it.

So I worked my way back up to second-string quarterback in 1952, the year we went 11–0 and had invitations to three bowl games, Orange, Sugar, and Cotton. It was our choice, coach Dodd told us. Then a strange thing happened. The seniors decided they were going to ask for a lot of fringe benefits, tickets, and expense money and such, and, as usual, they convinced the rest of the squad. You might say it was a veiled strike threat, no benefits, no bowl. I didn't care about all that stuff. I had had a pretty good season. My field goal beat Florida, 17–14, and I had done well in beating arch-rival Georgia, 23–9.

When the seniors presented their demands, coach Dodd was about as mad as I've ever seen him.

"Let me tell you one thing," he said, "I'm going to give you exactly the same thing I gave you last year, no less, no more. And if you don't want to go to a bowl game, just let me know because I'd rather go fishing anyway."

With that he stormed off. But not far. We ran after him and told him that we had reconsidered. So we went to the Sugar Bowl and played Ole Miss, a team coach Dodd didn't want to play. He wanted to play Syracuse in the Orange Bowl. We had a tough time against Ole Miss, but finally won out, 24–7, and I kicked a field goal and threw a touchdown pass. Alabama beat Syracuse by 50 or 60 points in the Orange Bowl.

That was my junior year.

When I arrived for my senior year, the news was disastrous. The college rulemakers had eliminated two-platoon football and now everyone was expected to play both ways, offense and defense—and I had no experience, none whatsoever, on defense. I'd never made a tackle except in self-defense. But since I had risen to be the starting quarterback, I wasn't going to let the opportunity slide by, and I applied myself on defense and was playing fairly well until I was injured just before the season started. I returned in the third game of the season against SMU, and the best thing I did was get tackled for a safety, and back to the bench I went as we beat Tulane and Auburn to run our unbeaten streak to 31 games. It all ended the next week at South Bend, Indiana, where Notre Dame beat us, 27–13, in a game in which their coach, Frank Leahy, collapsed at half time and was hospitalized.

All the while I was plotting to regain my job. Then it came to me. Vanderbilt, our next opponent, was one of the weaker teams on our schedule, and I knew I would get a chance to play in relief.

I needed to do something spectacular.

In order to carry out my plan, I needed the help of Colonel Danforth and his sports column. So during the days preceding the game, I asked Danforth if he knew the record for consecutive passes completed in a Southeastern Conference game. He said twelve.

"Well, Colonel Danforth, if I get into the game against Vanderbilt next Saturday, I am going to break that record," I said.

He laughed. Colonel Danforth always liked me.

The script had been set. The rest of the plan was this: When I got into the game, I was going to throw a screen pass left, screen pass right, screen left, screen right . . . 13 screen passes . . . and break the record. It was almost a foolproof plan.

Sure enough we got an early lead, and I trotted in the Vandy game to implement the Rodgers Grand Plan. I threw screen left, screen right, screen left, and I was rocking right along when I got cocky and threw a hook pass and missed it. But I did hit three touchdown passes and win the starting quarterback job for the last four games of my senior year, Clemson, Alabama, Duke, and Georgia. We finished up 9–2 and accepted an invitation to play West Virginia in the Sugar Bowl.

The moment had come, my final game, and I took advantage of it. West Virginia had a couple of guys named Sam Huff and Bruce Bosley, who later became all-Pros, but we won, 42–19, when I passed for three touchdowns and kicked a field goal.

When things are going good, you can't miss. On one play I overthrew a halfback and an end downfield caught the pass.

"Weren't you throwing to me?" the halfback asked me when he got back to the huddle.

"Man, you think I'm that bad a passer?" I said.

So, after three years of varsity football, I had closed out

each with a big afternoon in a major bowl and kicked at least one field goal in each and been named Most Valuable Player of the 1954 Sugar Bowl, which I thought was pretty nifty.

But more than that, I had left them applauding.

In looking back over my college days, I reflect on the influence Bobby Dodd had on my life. I couldn't tell you how many games he won at Georgia Tech, but I can tell you what he did for me. He gave me a chance to play the game, he taught me the fundamentals and a coaching style, and to a large degree, he is responsible for what success I attain.

Chapter V

Somebody Always Makes Those
              Right Turns for Me

Bobby Dodd always said if you believe you are lucky, you will be. He was a positive thinker before it became profitable to be one. Luck or timing or fate or whatever means a lot to me, and I have always been prepared to offer a push, a helping hand, or whatever it takes to activate it. I would add a qualification. Luck is more likely to find those who are prepared.

Many people mope around and gripe that they haven't had a chance in life, yet when the train of opportunity made stop after stop they failed to board. Sometimes you get one chance, sometimes you get many.

At Brown High School I had to give fate a hand. I talked coach J. E. DeVaughn into shifting Charlie Brannon, a better athlete, to halfback so I could play quarterback. Brannon could play a lot of positions, I couldn't.

At Georgia Tech I did not start a single season as the No. 1 quarterback for one reason or other—I was hurt my senior year—but I finished each as a bowl game hero who kicked a field goal or threw a touchdown pass. After sitting out most of my senior year, I plotted to regain the starting job in the Vanderbilt game and I did, finishing up the last four games and being named MVP in the Sugar Bowl. This is not mentioned as a matter of vanity but, rather, to illustrate that a person should be prepared to enter when the door is opened.

But there is also fate, pure fate, a mysterious door-opening outside the realm of human endeavor. As I look back, I can see turns in the road where I could have gone one way or another in the life of Pepper Rodgers. My wish was to be a coach, but before I could be a coach, I had to be a flier, which I didn't want to be.

Somehow, fate was always there.

Let's go back to my senior year at Georgia Tech. We had gone to New Orleans to play Tulane, and New Orleans wasn't the easiest place for a young man to play football because of the temptations of Bourbon Street, the carnival atmosphere, the bars, the music, and the girls. A coach can't lock up all his players, and yet he doesn't want to lose a game on Bourbon Street.

Coach Dodd was aware of the dilemma. Before the trip he called us together and laid out the regulations. Coach Dodd was far ahead of his time, a lenient coach in certain ways but in complete control. He could have made the transition from the "old days" to modern football without any trouble. He knew people. He knew that prohibiting drinking would only lead to drinking behind locked doors.

"Two glasses of wine, that's all you can have in New

Orleans," he said to us. "I don't want to hear of anyone having more."

The flesh proved weaker than the rules. Several of us had two glasses, then three, then more.

On the Monday following the game I was called to coach Dodd's office.

"Pepper, did you have more than two glasses of wine?" he asked.

I never lied to coach Dodd.

"Yes, sir."

"You are suspended from the team for one day and deprived of your complimentary ticket privileges."

"Yes, sir."

Coach Dodd gave me a second chance. If he had not, I would not be the head coach at Georgia Tech today. Fate. And a lesson learned. A coach can take the hard line and suspend players for minor infractions and withdraw scholarships and send them home, or, as I believe, he can leave that up to the school. A school takes away scholarships; I coach the football team. Give a kid a second chance and it could be the factor that motivates and matures him. When I was an undergraduate, I used to take the tennis net to the courts for coach Dodd and assistant coach Frank Broyles. If I hadn't gotten a second chance, I might still be lugging that damn net.

That was the first hand of fate.

After I played out my eligibility at Georgia Tech, I served as a student assistant coach in 1954. I knew what I wanted to do. I wanted to coach. But there was a major obstacle, the Korean War, and as an officer in ROTC I faced an obligation. This was a source of great resentment for a young coach anxious to begin a career, and I had this on my mind the next spring when I was invited to the University of Virginia to help Ned McDonald put in the belly series made famous by coach Dodd. This resentment grew when I was recalled to Atlanta after two weeks and inducted into the Air Force.

I felt cheated. McDonald had offered me a permanent position on his staff. This depression followed me when I reported for duty at Spence Air Force Base Flying School in South Georgia. I began thinking of ways to get out. Only one seemed foolproof.

I would say my wife, Judy, was deathly afraid of my flying. Naturally I was too much of a man, a Southern gentleman, and a football player to say that for myself. So I used my wife and two children as an excuse. The commanding officer was sympathetic and promised to wait around and see what happened before making a decision. Confident that I would be sprung from service, I spent weekends in Atlanta watching Georgia Tech home games. I knew what I wanted to do. I wanted to coach at Virginia.

On one of those trips to Atlanta my car broke down at Moultrie, Georgia, and I had it towed to a garage where I ran into an old friend, Jerry Beers, a Tech man and a Coca-Cola official who was on a hunting trip to South Georgia.

"What are you doing these days?" he asked.

"I'm in flying school at Spence."

"Good. When do you get your wings?"

"Three or four months."

I felt lousy when I returned to Spence that night. I knew if I was ashamed to tell Jerry Beers what I was doing, it was wrong. I didn't have the guts to tell him I was quitting. The next morning I dashed down to the commanding officer's office and told him I'd changed my mind.

Now, for irony and fate. A short time later McDonald was fired at Virginia and replaced by Ben Martin. It was like a checkerboard of life. From Spence I was sent to Hamilton Air Force Base in Texas, and Martin eventually ended up as the head coach at the Air Force Academy in Denver.

He looked around in the service for a coach and a Virginia assistant recommended me and suddenly I was doing what I wanted to do, coach. If I had gotten out of the Air Force and taken the job with McDonald, I would have been just another unemployed assistant coach.

Being in the Air Force was not easy for someone who did not like flying. It was hard on me. But then so was football. Playing football was hard for a guy who didn't like the contact. I made it in football because I concentrated on the game and the strategy.

After two years at the Air Force Academy, I realized I preferred the civilian life. Ray Graves, who had recruited me at Georgia Tech, had just taken the head coaching job at the University of Florida, and when he offered me a job coaching the offensive backfield, I took it.

Ben Martin was upset that I didn't tell him I preferred being a civilian.

"We could have worked it out," he said. "You could

have coached here at the Air Force Academy as a civilian."

He had never told me that. Conversely, I had never asked. I have thought of that conversation many times in the intervening years and how many problems of the world can be traced to lack of communications. So much is left unsaid. We don't tell our mothers and fathers we appreciate them until it's too late. We don't tell our wives we love them. Our society is afraid to express emotions.

If too much was left unsaid at the Air Force Academy, too much was said at Florida—rumors, innuendo, outright falsehoods. I was blamed for things I had no control over. Suffice it to say that in my fifth year Graves was ready to unload me to relieve the pressure on the overall program. Not that he had anything against me personally. He liked me, I know that. But he felt I had become a burden. I was too controversial and he did not want that.

Nothing was orthodox at Florida.

The way I learned I was to be fired was most unconventional.

Ed Kensler, another assistant coach, told me in a Baton Rouge hotel before our last game with LSU.

"Pepper, you know you're going to be fired," he said.

No, I didn't know it. I had been controversial and highly visible, true, but I didn't know the breach was that advanced. But then the victim is usually the last to know he is to be fired. Graves dreaded confrontations and I guess he was awaiting the opportune moment. Finally, he summoned me. He said Alabama assistant Gene Stallings had taken the head coaching job at Texas A&M, and he would be most pleased to recommend me as a member of his new staff. That is not as nasty as firing someone outright.

"But I like it here at Florida," I said, and he winced.

But this would open new horizons for me.

"Ray, if you're trying to get rid of me, I'll go. But I like Florida. I don't want to go to Texas A&M."

He was forced to postpone the separation, but I did not need a calendar to remind me my days at Florida were numbered.

Graves had hinted that if I hadn't found another job by the time of the Coaches Convention, I would be uncoupled from the staff. His eyes lit up when I told him that Oregon State coach Tommy Prothro asked me out to the West Coast for an interview. He was preparing his team for the Rose Bowl game. This would resolve the problem for Graves without a confrontation.

A funny thing happened in California. Prothro offered me a job, not at Oregon State, but at UCLA. He had already taken the job at UCLA, but the announcement wasn't to be made until after the Rose Bowl game.

He put it on the line, the most honest approach I had encountered.

"I need a quarterback coach to sit in the press box and call the offense," he said. "At Oregon State I do that, but I won't be able to continue this method at UCLA. Pepper, I hear you're a good coach. I don't know that. If at the end of one year I decide you can't do the job, I'll give you another year to relocate."

I liked that. No doubletalk.

There was one stipulation. I couldn't tell anyone until after the Rose Bowl game.

Upon my return to Gainesville, I found Graves most anxious to learn details of the interview.

"Did you take the job at Oregon State?" he asked.

"No," I said.

His jaws fell. But it was the truth. I didn't take the job at Oregon State. I took the job at UCLA, but because of my promise to Prothro, I couldn't tell anyone, not even Graves.

On a morning soon thereafter, when I arrived in my office, I found an envelope. Inside was a yellow legal sheet. There was a message. It read, "Pepper, you're fired."

I would imagine that Graves was most surprised when the announcement came out that I was going to UCLA. As I see it, as negative as it might have seemed at the time, this too was the hand of fate.

The irony is that I got fired and got a two thousand dollar raise.

Prothro had offered me a salary of $12,000 a year and I told him I made that much at Florida. What I didn't say was that I wouldn't be making that much very much longer. So he checked with school officials and said he could get me $14,000.

I thought that was pretty courageous of me, a guy without a job, to ask for a two thousand dollar raise.

We had two highly successful years at UCLA, beat SC twice, and when the Kansas head coaching job opened up, I was asked to Lawrence for an interview. I had not applied for the job. From what I understand, Kansas officials were interviewing Darrell Mudra and asked if he knew any other prospect, and he had mentioned me. I had given my first football clinic at a small school where he was the head coach. Tommy Prothro also gave me a recommendation.

So I was interviewed and hired on the same day.

Four years later, in 1970, Prothro resigned at UCLA to succeed George Allen as head coach of the Los Angeles Rams of the National Football League, and I was named to succeed him.

Once more, the hand of fate. If I had not been fired at Florida, I never would have gone to the West Coast to coach under Prothro, and if I had not worked for Prothro, I would not have gotten the Kansas and UCLA jobs.

The road always leads back home, it seems, and in 1974 I ended up where I had started, at Georgia Tech, where Bobby Dodd gave me that second chance in 1953 after I had had more than two glasses of wine at New Orleans.

That's it, fate. And a whole lot of pushing, shoving, and brashness.

1. To my mother, Louise, who wanted me to be a tap dancer or a musician, I was quite the dude, even at age four.

2. My father, Franklin, figured he had a budding Ty Cobb in 1941 when I was ten.

3. Here I am at Brown High School in 1948 holding my future—a football.

4. At long last, ol' Rodgers becomes a hero with his last-minute, winning field goal in the January 1952 Orange Bowl game between Georgia Tech and Baylor.

5. Here's a close-up of me, the quarterback who, they said, "couldn't do anything but win."

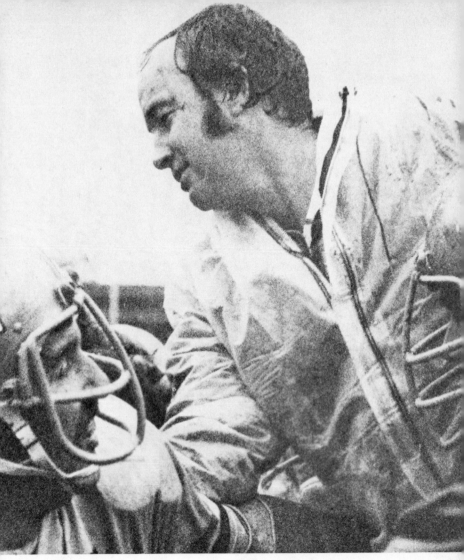

6. Twenty years after I left Georgia Tech as a student, I returned for this victory ride on November 30, 1974, following our 34–14 upset over arch-rival Georgia at Athens.

7. A blackboard is a coach's alter ego. That's where it all starts. (*Dwight Ross, Jr., Atlanta Journal-Constitution Photo.*)

8. If Bobby Dodd, here sharing a joke with me, had not understood the ways of youth, I would not be where I am today, in his old job.

Chapter VI   *A Red Baron in the Wild Blue
                Yonder I Wasn't*

I never wanted to fly. I wanted to be a pilot, wear the
wings, the scarf, be the hero, be something others could
not be. On the other hand, I wanted to be a football
coach. But, as a philosopher once said, you can't have everything. Ben Martin gave me the opportunity to coach at
the Air Force Academy and, as a commissioned officer in
the Air Force, I wore the wings, the scarf, and was something others could not be.

Unfortunately, I also had to fly.

Evidently some little angel up in the clouds was looking after me. Otherwise, the wide, wide world of sports
and Pepper Rodgers would never have merged. Flying
was not natural for me, but then neither was playing football. I did both because of ego.

Let's explore this ego thing. When I was a student at
Georgia Tech, my goal was to be the first-string quarterback. In 1955 my goal was to be named an assistant coach
at Virginia. In 1956 in Moultrie, Georgia, class of 56-S at

Spence Air Force Base, my goal was simply to survive as a pilot.

I survived my first flying crisis that same year.

Let me set the scene. A somewhat pale Pepper Rodgers, unrecognized by the plane as a hero of three bowls, is struggling with the controls for the first time in South Georgia and the civilian instructor, Mr. Ross, is bored at the prospect of coddling another frightened neophyte. He tells me to "find the field" and then "shoot a stall." I feel more like finding a gun and shooting myself.

Finding the field means just what it says, you find the landing strip, and that is not as easy as it sounds with most terrain looking the same. Then you "shoot a stall." You pull the throttle back, mash the button, point to the instructor and say, "Level 75 turning base, gear down, three in the green, pressure's up, touch and go landing," or words to that effect. Plus, hold the damn thing level. All at the same time.

So I spill it out.

"Level 75 turning base, gear down, three in the green, pressure's up, touch and go landing."

Now, if your landing gear is not down, a horn goes off and alerts you that something is wrong.

Now I'm turning and I'm so excited I've got it lined up with the strip and I haven't crashed and I've kept it level so that I don't hear the horn. And from the ground they're shooting all kinds of flares at me and I think it is some kind of recognition for excellence.

Mr. Ross, getting a bit edgy, screams at me, "Lieutenant Rodgers, what do you do when the horn goes off?"

"Oh, I know, Mr. Ross," I said, "you reach over like this and press the button and turn it off."

I pressed the button and turned it off. He almost died. We almost died before he managed to get the gear down. I received a rather pointed lecture from Mr. Ross after the touch and go.

In all honesty, I don't see how the Air Force survived Pepper Rodgers.

The second of many crises came at Hamilton Air Force Base in Texas, where I had another forgettable experience on my first solo flight in a T-33 single-engine jet. Talk about ego! I envisioned myself as the Red Baron as I mounted the plane. I had that hat on, a scarf around my neck, the picture of a blasé air ace as I began to taxi out, make a sharp turn and take off. On the T-33 you released the throttle friction as you taxied, then tightened it before take-off. Unhappily, on those planes there was a non-steerable nose wheel, and occasionally it would get cocked like those old tricycle wheels. A tap on the brakes straightened it out.

Anyway, here comes the old air ace, and he makes a sharp turn and the nose wheel gets cocked and I'm going around in circles, making 360-degree turns with that jet engine whining, and I'm trying to remember what the manual said about all this, and then I hear a voice from the tower.

"Jet, 921976, having a little trouble?" he asks.

"Negative, 921976," I say, "just flying off for take-off."

I am still going around like a dog chasing his tail, and the cool, confident air ace is beginning to crumble into a mass of panic. I am sweating like mad and I've got the top down and my face mask off and wondering what in the hell to do. Somehow, perhaps accidentally, I tap the brakes and the nose straightens out and off I go into the wild blue yonder, not checking the throttle friction or anything. I pour the coals to it and hope that no one noticed my humiliating spins. I must be doing 400 miles an hour before I can get the gear up. Everytime I reach for the gear, the untightened throttle friction slips and I must grab it.

That comes close to being my most embarrassing moment.

It is not hard to be a football player when you are 6-4 and 250 pounds, and it is not hard to be a pilot when you love flying. What is hard is to be a pilot and survive five years because you want to wear the wings. People used to say to me I looked like I was having a good time and my answer was, "I have a good time when I am not flying." When I got to that plane, I was very, very serious. If I hadn't been serious and had pushed myself too far, I'd be dead.

Same way in coaching. I prepare myself and when I get on the field I am ready. I do the best I can. Off the field, I try not to replay games and have second thoughts. In this respect, Ben Martin, my first boss at the Air Force Academy, was a major influence in my life.

Of all the coaches I worked for, he had the healthiest on-the-field day-of-the-game approach and manner. After he had done everything in the world to win, he didn't worry about whether he had lost by a single point or three touchdowns. He was not hung up on statistics and figures and impressing the critics and alumni. He let the kids play the game and he was the perfect coach for a service academy. And once a game ended he insisted there was nothing anyone could do to alter the outcome and it was foolish to make those around us—wives, girl friends, office personnel, relatives—miserable. A lot of people are not for you unless you win. That's different. I am not talking about them. I mean those close to you. We shouldn't take out frustrations on them.

I become a bit suspicious when I hear or read that a coach burns the midnight oils or works into the early morning hours. Ben Martin never called a night meeting. When coaches say they meet until 3 or 4 A.M., what are they talking about? At Florida we used to hold those weary meetings just to discuss whether we were going to serve bacon or sausage for the team breakfasts. Night meetings are a smokescreen for coaches trying to convince hostile alumni they are working hard.

I consider myself fortunate I played at Georgia Tech under Bobby Dodd, where football was fun, and started my coaching career at Air Force under Ben Martin, where football was fun. When the tedium of practice wore on nerves, Ben always had a change of pace. Once he showed up with ten hoola hoops and coaches held a contest for the amusement of the players.

During my first spring practice—the school had just been moved from Denver to Colorado Springs—we had a staggering total of twenty-six players, hardly enough for a lively scrimmage. But there was a distinct advantage to being an infant school. We didn't have a single cadet who had graduated, therefore no alumni, therefore no alumni pressure. Our players were bright and articulate, and in Richie Mayo we had an extremely talented quarterback.

Before our first game, against the University of Detroit, everyone was on edge because we were anxious to make a good impression. It didn't help that our dressing room was next to the Detroit locker room and we could hear their growling and yelling and noises that tend to make opponents quiver in their cleats. As they thundered out to the field, sounding like a herd of mad bulls, our dressing room was as silent as the gallows.

That is, until Ben smiled and said, "Sounds like a hell of crap game going on in there."

He had perfect timing. Jitters turned to laughter, and we went out and won a football game.

There isn't a respectable football fan alive who doesn't recall that Notre Dame tied Iowa, 14–14, in 1953 when Frank Varrichone feigned an injury that bought the Irish some desperately needed seconds on their last drive. But how many remember that in 1958 an outmanned Air Force team tied Iowa, 13–13, when the Hawkeyes were the No. 1 ranked team in the country? That is not exactly accurate. We didn't tie Iowa. Iowa TIED US. And they had to go 99 yards in the last 6 minutes of the game to do it.

Point is, with our light brigade, our thin ranks, we didn't belong in the same stadium with an Iowa team that had such great players as Randy Duncan, Willie Fleming, and Bob Jeter. Yet we had the game won and were on their 1-yard line with 6 minutes to play. In my mind that has to be one of the greatest collegiate football efforts of all time.

Our return to Colorado Springs and a welcome by cheering cadets and townspeople was almost as exciting as the game. Following military protocol, we deplaned by rank and, lo and behold, the third or fourth officer off the plane was a "gorilla." It seems in our celebrating and drinking, an officer had put on this Halloween mask and neglected to remove it.

That wasn't so bad except there he was on the front page of the local newspaper the next day. Our hangovers were nothing compared to his.

That first year at the Air Force Academy we were un-defeated, with a couple of ties and a Cotton Bowl game with TCU, and I was beginning to think there was noth-ing to this coaching business. It was a snap.

But I was unprepared for the school's monastic ap-proach to the bowl game at Dallas. Where I had played my college football, bowl games were fun and lively trips, so it came as somewhat of a shock when Colonel George Simler, our athlete director, rationed out game tickets, one to a coach, and transportation tickets, one to a coach, and announced no wives or families would be permitted to accompany team personnel. Presumably, this was to as-sure dedication and celibacy.

But all wasn't lost. For recreation, we were allowed to play touch football, the ROTCs against the Ring-knockers, or West Point graduates.

Colonel Simler, who set national speed records, was a

fearless, swashbuckling pilot. He didn't fool around with a plane; he gave it orders. What bothered me was that planes didn't take orders. He didn't fool around with challenges either. He took them head-on. Like the bet that he couldn't take off with a full load on a hot day from the local strip where a plane had crashed a day earlier.

"Rodgers, we can do it," he said to me.

I smiled weakly. There I was, the reluctant pilot, trapped again.

He loaded me in the plane and we were hitting 200 miles an hour on the ramp before we hit the runway. That's why I never wanted to fly. We made it. But later George Simler was killed on take-off in Texas.

Being around all these men of derring-do, I guess I got a mite cocky myself. I had flown Ben Martin to Arizona, and we were returning to Colorado Springs when he informed me another plane was descending a few hundred feet way.

"Watch me," I said, throwing the scarf around my neck, "I'll beat that bastard down."

I landed just ahead of the other pilot and Ben swore he would never fly with me again. But that was the Air Force Academy, a thrill a minute.

At the end of my second year in Colorado Springs I got restless for the civilian life. Not that I didn't like the Academy, I did. But work was too much like civil service in which you had to put in a specified amount of time before you advanced. And I was tired of being the last officer off the plane.

My chance came when Ray Graves, who had recruited

me at Georgia Tech, became head coach at Florida in 1960 and offered me the backfield coaching job. I accepted.

My leaving was worth it just to attend the farewell party, or dining-in, as we called it. It was some bash, starting with wine toasts by lieutenants, then captains, and on up the line. By the time we got to the commander in chief, everybody was hanging from the rafters. The honored guests, those leaving, were then handed a drink called the Green Death, a concoction of every brand at the bar, and ordered to chug-a-lug. As I downed mine, I was serenaded by . . .

> Oh, here's Pepper, he's true blue,
> He's a drunkard, through and through.
> He's a bastard, so they say.
> He'll never get to heaven,
> So he went the other way.
> So drink, chug-a-lug, chug-a-lug . . .

I drank two Green Deaths and, really, that's all I remember. Later someone told me that in a game of leap-frog, I tried to hurdle ten men and I climbed the bar and held on to the chandelier. The party broke up when Tom Berry made a swan dive off the mantel and broke a colonel's leg.

Even in mirth, though, there was sadness. My best friend at the Academy, Tom Baake, a fellow assistant coach, did not attend the party because his wife was in labor at the hospital. She died in childbirth. Five years later Tom crashed and died on take-off at Cocoa, Florida.

I'll never forget Tom Baake for he had saved my life on one of the many flights we made together. We were hanging over thunderstorm clouds at forty thousand feet when I, failing to put my oxygen on pressure demand, slipped into unconsciousness. Next thing I knew we were diving through the thunderstorm and Tom was shouting at me to put my controls on emergency.

"You were out," he said to me when we leveled off.

Strange thing, when you go out for lack of oxygen you never know it. In one simulated test we had an instructor jerk away the oxygen from pilots playing cards. When oxygen was restored, they played the next card as if nothing had happened.

Anyway, in 1960, Pepper Rodgers, reluctant pilot, left the Air Force Academy and resumed civilian life at the University of Florida. It was to be five stormy years.

Chapter VII   *Hurricane Land and Ole*
                  Pepper in the Eye

Like sophomores and losing, firing is a fact of coaching life. Some have been fired more than others.

I have been fired twice in my life. Not a bad average. But I'll bet no one has been fired exactly like Pepper Rodgers. The first time, as guy just out of college, I was fired on a tennis court. The next time—last, I hope—I was fired by a yellow legal sheet placed in an envelope and left on my desk.

My first uncoupling was rather amusing. It was the year after I played out my eligibility at Georgia Tech, and while waiting to see what my service status was I accepted a job with a newly formed magazine, *Sports Unlimited, Inc.*, founded and edited by a couple of close newspaper friends, Jim Minter and Jack Jackson. They had borrowed a thousand dollars and entered the publishing field. And I was hired, at a salary of $100 a week to sell ads. Those guys knew a salesman when they saw one, and their faith in me was reinforced when I returned the first day with an ad. Super salesman Rodgers wasted no time. I scurried downtown and sold an ad to an old friend, Tommy Reeder, proprietor of a sporting goods store. That impressed Minter and Jackson. I figured a quick start would aid my cause. Unbeknownst to them, Reeder was my first and last prospect.

I overestimated the value of a one-sale salesman. Three weeks later, still enjoying the immense success of my career and realizing that all work and no play made Pepper a dull boy, I arranged a tennis match with Frank Broyles, my old Tech backfield coach. Usually my timing was impeccable. This time it was atrocious. As the fates would have it, Minter and Jackson motored past the court and I detected a look of agitation on their faces. Oh, well, they knew their super salesman needed to relax, and perhaps they thought I was working on a big deal with Broyles.

So I went back to the game, which was close. So close, in fact, that it lasted three hours and that was my undoing. Three hours later Minter and Jackson rode by again and there I was hitting the tennis ball. Ping, ping, pong, pong . . . gone.

Pepper Rodgers was unemployed, fired.

Ten years later—I am one of those guys fired only once every decade—I fell victim again at the University of Florida. And as I look back, I see another tennis connection. Ray Graves, another former tennis partner, lowered the boom this time. There should be a moral there somewhere. This time, though, I was fired by letter, not face-to-face.

Ray Graves really didn't want to fire me, but I had become too controversial, and he didn't want controversy.

Sure, in my stay at Florida, from 1960 to 1964, I made mistakes. Graves, in his first head coaching job, made some, too. But that is all part of the football game.

Florida was good for me. That might sound strange to you. I say that because in Gainesville I experienced everything there is to experience in coaching in a state where there are as many alumni factions as there are football prospects, and there are many, many prospects.

The first thing we had to do at Florida was put together a football team with two quarterbacks, 5-8, 138-pound Larry Libertore and Bobby Dodd, Jr., son of Graves' former boss and my former head coach. That in itself was an explosive situation. Somehow we had to utilize the talents of both. Libertore was a slippery runner, good on sprintouts, and Dodd was the superior passer and ball handler. I recall that when asked if he'd like his son to play for him at Georgia Tech, coach Dodd said no and explained why. He said if Bobby, Jr., were a great quarterback or a poor quarterback, he would like him to play at Tech, but since he was somewhere in-between, a father-son situation would be too controversial. Well, as it turned out, we at Florida got all the heat.

Our careers at Florida got off to a roaring start. In one of our earlier games, it was disclosed a gambler had approached our fullback, Jon McBeth, about fixing a score. McBeth reported this to authorities, and the guy was sent up the river.

Then the next week we had another interesting game, Florida versus Georgia Tech at Gainesville. The angles were too numerous to mention, but for starters consider:

father vs. son, coach vs. former assistants, wife and mother divided. It was something. I liked what Alice Dodd said, "I hope Bobby, Jr., has a good day and Georgia Tech wins." That way she did not take sides against her son or husband.

No one in Hollywood could have written a script like that game in 1960. The finish was even more unreal.

We go into the fourth quarter trailing Tech, 17–10, and things are looking bad for the home team. Facing a critical fourth-down play, we send Bobby, Jr., into the game for a pass, and he rifles one to Don Deal for 32 yards to the Georgia Tech 25-yard line. Then he sneaks for a crucial first down and recovers a fumble that keeps the drive going. With Libertore and Dodd sharing in the quarterbacking, it is a suspenseful race against the clock.

Once more, at the Georgia Tech 4-yard line, we face a critical fourth down with 2 yards to go. Now it is Libertore's turn, and he pitches out to Lindy Infante and we score with 32 seconds left in the game. Now the score is 17–16, and we can kick an extra point and tie the game or go for 2 and win if we make it. We call a time out and, deciding that we have used up all the plays in our repertoire, I make one up. I tell Libertore to fake McBeth into the line, then roll out and throw to him in the deepest corner of the end zone. Tech goes for the fake and McBeth catches the ball and we win, 18–17.

During that drive, I know the person who suffered the most was Alice Dodd. She wanted Bobby, Jr., to do well, yet she did not want Tech to lose. A reporter who sat next to her quoted her as cheering when Bobby, Jr., dropped back to pass. "Hit him, honey!" Then she said, "That was a pretty good pass, wasn't it? I'm rooting for my team, Georgia Tech, but I'm rooting for my No. 1 boy, too. I've learned you can pull two or three ways at the same time." Not many mothers have been in the predicament that Alice Dodd was in that afternoon.

It was a very emotional football game.

Thereafter my relationship with Georgia Tech began to deteriorate. I don't mean to imply the game had anything to do with it. It didn't. But it is not easy to coach the son of a famous person and especially one close to you. This held true for Graves, too. And, being young and aggressive, I made recruiting mistakes. In my zeal to recruit some boys, I said things like Georgia Tech was on a downward course. It was just a ploy, and I know I shouldn't have said it. That's one thing I tell my assistants and recruiters today, never ridicule or knock the other schools. Let the boy make an honest choice.

That first season at Florida was a very good one for us. We went 8-2 and beat Baylor in the Gator Bowl. So far, in two assistant coaching jobs, I had had two great break-in seasons. At the Air Force we were unbeaten; at Florida, we lost only two.

Coaching indeed seemed like an easy job. But things were to change, and for a brief morning on Friday, April 14, 1961, football seemed very insignificant to me. The day started just like any other fishing excursion into the Gulf of Mexico off Tampa. Five Florida coaches, Jack Green, John Donaldson, Jim Powell, Jimmy Dunn, and I met Ray Ellis, a Tampa television executive and former

Georgia Tech assistant, at the Tampa Bay Marina for a day of fun in the sun.

Soon we were settled on board a 40-foot Chris Craft, the *Hi-Way*, under the direction of Captain Bill Black, for an all-day assault on kingfish mixed in with a few tall tales and a little beer drinking.

Three and a half hours later, or at approximately 11 A.M., we stared into the face of death. We were trolling for kingfish, I from the back of the boat, when it happened. The whole thing went up in an explosion. Even now it is difficult to piece together what happened. As Captain Black told it later, "I turned on the switch and hit the starter button and it blew. It knocked out all the windows and glass was everywhere and there was fire all over. The engine hatches were blown off and I was knocked on one of the motors, out cold."

All I could remember was being hit and lifted by this explosion. The impact knocked me back on top of a motor and I felt my clothes on fire and my skin burning. The whole damn place was on fire. I knew I had to do something, get away, get away from the fire. The water, the water, I thought, get to the water. So I forced myself up and dived overboard.

Jack Green was already there.

"I'm okay, Pepper, don't try to save me," he said to me.

"I'm not trying to save you, Jack, I'm trying to save myself," I said.

Strange the thoughts you have at such a time. I thought of my five years in the Air Force and the close shaves I had had and my survival and the bone-jarring collisions I had had with all those defensive tackles in football and how I had managed to live through those, and here I was close to an ignominious death on a beautiful fishing day in the Gulf of Mexico. Bleeding, burned, my mind addled, I was suddenly fearful sharks would follow the scent of blood and pull me under. It was the most unbelievable feeling in the world.

Fortunately, John Donaldson was not near the explosion and had the presence of mind to grab a life preserver and look for Jimmy Dunn, who could not swim. This kept Jimmy afloat until we were rescued. Later John gave his description of the blast: "I heard one thud, then a helluva roar—the boat rocked sideways and flames shot out all over the cockpit. I could see Pepper and he looked bad. He was down in the engine compartment on top of the engine and all of his clothes were burning. Then he scrambled up and jumped overboard."

We swam, a mile, a half-mile, a hundred yards, I don't know how far. Some complained later that many boaters fishing in the area just watched and made no move toward coming to our aid. I don't know about that. I do know that Donald Davidson, enjoying the first day in his 23-foot boat, *Al-Mar*, pulled up and brought four of us aboard. Three young boys in a kicker boat picked up the captain and the others. We never did get their names.

Captain Black was in the most vulnerable position, as he told us later. "I was out, but the fire woke me up," he said. "I couldn't get overboard. I was hurt, my leg was hurting so bad I didn't think I could get over the side, but the heat got so intense I made myself go over into the water."

Once ashore, I felt terrible, cold yet fully aware of the burns on my face and arms. I turned to Jack Green. "Jack, how do I look?" I asked. He said, "You look all right."

That might seem like an insignificant statement to some, but I'll always remember Jack Green and thank him because he represented strength. When you're burned, in pain, and think you might die, you need somebody like that.

The casualty report read like something out of a war zone. I had first-, second-, and third-degree burns of the arms, face, and legs; Powell had second- and third-degree burns of the eyes, head, both hands, arms, and legs; Ellis had first- and second-degree burns of the entire body, Green had first-degree burns of the face and hands, Dunn had first-degree burns of the face and second-degree burns of the right hand, and Donaldson had first-degree burns of the face and right hand.

A friend came to the hospital and asked how I was feeling and I said "great" and he thought I was crazy. But everything was relative. When I got to the hospital and found out I was going to survive, I felt a lot better than when I was twelve miles out in the Gulf and on fire.

Now I could be my flip self again. When someone consoled me, I said, "Better me than Libertore—he's important to the team, I'm not."

I was told there were sharks in the area and my answer

was, "If you're in an explosion and don't get killed, you're burned and survive, you jump in the water and don't drown; then, if a shark gets you, it's just not your day."

Still, it was a sobering experience, and I was reminded of a bit of philosophy served up by my service station man. He said work every day like you're to live forever and live every day like you're going to die tomorrow.

Think about that. I have often.

For obvious reasons, since that April morning in 1961, I have never considered football a life-and-death matter.

It would be accurate to say the remainder of my time at Florida was shrouded in controversy, primarily over quarterbacks but including other facets of the game such as field strategy.

We didn't have much of a year in 1961. We lost a lot of players academically, and Graves, being new in the head coaching business, made a diplomatic error when he said it was only a matter of time before they returned. This kind of talk did not exactly please the faculty. We also lost a couple of players who confessed to lopping off the tail of the mascot alligator.

But even in adversity we had a little fun, especially in the Tulane game when I resurrected the old sleeper play in a 14–3 victory. The way it worked, we sent in two substitutes and three players ran off, only one stopped on the sidelines. That player, Jim O'Donnell, then sprinted down the field and caught a touchdown pass from Bobby Dodd, Jr.

Libertore, who had been Sophomore of the Year in the

Southeastern Conference, was being better defensed the
second time around the league, and we finished with a
4-5-1 record.

The next year, 1962, we had a young left-handed sophomore quarterback in Tom Shannon who showed a lot of
promise. I liked him because he was a lot like I was at
Georgia Tech; confident, yea, even cocky. First we'd had
all that flak about Libertore and Dodd. And now, as
Shannon moved in as the starting quarterback, Libertore
was unhappy and bitter and some of the fans were
divided. Result: more controversy—with Rodgers in the
eye of the storm.

Well, we went 7-4, lost to Georgia Tech, 17–0, but beat
Penn State in the Gator Bowl, and Shannon was named
the most valuable player. Let me say here that I really admired Libertore. He did some fine things for us, returning
punts and such, and I knew how he felt, having spent
most of my Georgia Tech career on the bench.

Shannon had it all to himself in 1963 and we were
6-3-1. That year is memorable in that Shannon was in-
strumental in beating Alabama and Joe Namath in Tuscaloosa, 10–6. If my records are straight, Bear Bryant and
Alabama haven't lost in Tuscaloosa since.

Now, 1964, and we've got a sophomore quarterback by
the name of Steve Spurrier and he's threatening to get
into the lineup and there is a tug-of-war between quarterback factions in the state. Some want Shannon, others
want Spurrier. We start with Shannon and then switch to
Spurrier and now Shannon is unhappy and all kinds of rumors are circulating in the state about me.

Once more we go to Tuscaloosa and Spurrier has a great game against Namath, but we lose, 17–14, after rushing a field-goal attempt with no time outs and missing it. During the late stages of the game, Spurrier gets knocked a little dizzy and he thinks he is on the Alabama 2 instead of the 7 and tries a running play on third down before the aborted field-goal attempt. Denny Stadium is as quiet as a dropped pin when the horn sounds ending the game as Jimmy Hall's kick is up in the air. It is a little eerie.

As the season progressed, so did the heat on Rodgers. The quarterback shuttle was blamed on me. There was even a rumor after the Georgia game in Jacksonville that I had had a fist fight with 6-4, 219-pound Roger Pettee, a senior center. That was the most ridiculous thing I'd ever heard of. Why I wouldn't even fight 138-pound Larry Libertore, much less Roger Pettee.

But the tongues were wagging and there was no stopping them.

Then came the clincher, the first loss ever to Florida State in Tallahassee.

Florida State, which had a couple of fair country players in Steve Tensi and Fred Biletnikoff, led by fourteen points late in the fourth quarter. We scored to get within a touchtown, then tried an onside kick. They recovered it and went in for a field goal and now they were ten points ahead and out of reach.

I was blamed for the onside kick. First of all, I was not responsible for calling onside kicks, and if I had called it no one would have paid any attention. That is the head coach's domain. All of us who are head coaches realize that everything reflects on us; if we don't want to do it, it isn't done. Yet I was blamed for losing the first game to Florida State. I was so mad I could have cried.

Perhaps I should have gotten the message, but I didn't. I never suspected I was going to be fired until just before the last game of the season against LSU at Baton Rouge, when Ed Kensler, another assistant coach, tipped me off.

We beat LSU in a great game, and in the next week or so I got a call from Graves.

I have already mentioned he had this thing about personal confrontations and he tried an indirect approach.

"Pepper, Gene Stallings is leaving Alabama to become head coach at Texas A&M, and I think it would be a great opportunity for you to apply for his staff," he said. "I will give you a high recommendation."

I said, "Coach, do you want me to leave?"

He said it would be to my advantage.

I said, "I like it here at Florida."

He winced.

Later, he told me if I didn't have a job by the time of the annual Coaches Convention, he would be forced to let me go.

That was when I talked with Tommy Prothro and decided on UCLA, as I mentioned earlier.

I liked Ray Graves and he liked me, and I know he didn't want to fire me. But he felt I had become an albatross around his neck.

He has some good qualities and, like all of us, some bad

qualities. He was good at getting quality football players to come to Florida and good at promising them they would play no matter what. This was not very good for the assistants who had to coach them. They were put in pressurized situations. I mean, if I were coaching Steve Spurrier, Graves would do a good job of getting him, a great job of selling me, and I'd do a great job of selling Graves. That part of Graves was really sensational. But he tried too hard to please everyone, and that only causes you to please no one.

Like most of us he dreaded the thought of anyone telling him no, turning him down.

This really happened. He wanted to hire a defensive backfield coach. He got me to call Don James at Florida State, Ed Kensler called Bud Carson and Norm Carlson called Billy Kinard, three good men who were later head coaches. He had all three in for interviews, and each left thinking he had the job. When he had made up his mind, Graves sent telegrams to the losers. That was because he didn't want to make anyone mad face to face. You've got to admire that trait, but it can cause some problems.

Back earlier, when I was in favor, Graves called me aside outside his office one morning.

"Just wanted you to know," he said, "I've been up to the athletic board and recommended you as assistant head coach. But I must tell you that some board members are opposed to the idea because of your youth."

I told him I was flattered.

"But don't worry about it," I said. "You have older and

more deserving guys in Jack Green and Gene Ellenson. I've got plenty of time. But whatever you decide is fine with me."

I felt good about even the suggestion.

I was still in high spirits until that afternoon when I played golf with Norm Sloan, the Florida basketball coach, who in casual conversation said, "Did Ray tell you they are going to make Jack Green assistant head coach?"

"No, he didn't."

"Well, it's going to be announced in the morning papers."

"You're kiddin'. I just talked to Ray Graves and he said he recommended me."

So I ran into Graves that afternoon and confronted him.

I said, "You told me you were going to recommend me as assistant head coach. You didn't say anything about Jack Green."

Graves said, "I'm not going to make Jack Green assistant head coach."

Poor Jack Green. He woke up the next morning and found his title changed to administrative assistant.

Things like that were always happening at Florida. Gene Ellenson went up to Georgia to be interviewed for the head coaching job when Wally Butts retired. He didn't get the job because he said he'd like to start over with a new staff, and Georgia wanted to keep its assistant coaches. Anyway, when he returned to Florida he'd been switched from defensive chief to offensive coach.

Then later when Jack Green accepted the Vanderbilt

job and volunteered to return and help us prepare for the
Gator Bowl game, he was informed that Ellenson had
been shifted to his old job and he could help in another
capacity.

"I ain't coming back," Green said.

Still, in retrospect, I don't blame Ray Graves. Now, as a
head coach, I see you have to do some things that are not
popular. You have to hire and fire coaches, and it is not a
pleasant task. I am convinced he did not want to fire me.
He felt he had to.

Taking a positive outlook, it was probably the best
thing that could have happened to me. Five years as an
assistant coach in a small college town is not the way to
grow as a football coach unless you want to spend the rest
of your life there.

Chapter VIII   What, Me Block and Tackle?

I didn't think much of it when Tommy Prothro stood on the practice field that first day and said we would all coach the "UCLA way."

Coaches have different methods and different philosophies. That's what makes the game of football so interesting. Knute Rockne didn't coach like Bob Neyland, Fielding Yost didn't coach like Amos Alonzo Stagg.

So the "UCLA way"—couldn't be too bad.

Little did I realize what Pepper Rodgers had wrought for himself. The "UCLA way" meant coaches, all coaches, had to do everything the players did, like block and tackle and hit those infernal dummies.

I made a mild protest.

"Coach Prothro," I said, "I came here to coach the quarterbacks, not to block and tackle."

He was unfazed.

"Ev'erbody coaches this way at UCLA, Pa'pper," he said in that Prothroian drawl.

I thought I was going to die. Here I am hitting that

dummy and I am not doing it right and Prothro is stand-ing on my toe and making me roll off the ball of my foot. Hell, I never did that when I was playing football. As I have said many times, I was not a contact player. I was a thinker and a finesse man. But here I am at the age of thirty-four doing what I never did in high school. I am actually trying to make a tackle, make a block, and hit a dummy machine.

Terry Debay, who used to play for UCLA, saved my life. He gave me some advice.

I had brought my problems to him. "Terry," I said, "I'm not getting any pop into my hits on that damn machine, and Prothro keeps making me do it over and over."

He had the answer.

"I'll let you in on a secret," he said. "When you line up, think like a karate expert and when you plant your elbow into the machine give out one of those blood-curdling yells, like, 'ARRRRRGGGGGGHHHHHRRRRRR!' It sounds so much better."

The next day I line up and Prothro says, "Hokay, Pa'pper, let's see you get some pop into it."

Then I attack that machine, actually hitting it no harder than the day before, but I let out this scream that even scared me.

"AARRRRRRRGGGGGGHHHHHHRRRRR!"

That did the trick.

"That's a lot better, Pa'pper," Prothro said, mercifully moving on to the next coach.

Thereafter, each time I hit that monster I screamed to

the high heavens and Prothro, nodding approval, called for no reruns. To this day I don't know if I was fooling him or he was letting me off the hook. Whatever, I was not about to question it.

Tommy Prothro was the best coach I ever worked for, except for his eccentric idea of having ole Pepper block and tackle. His father, Doc Prothro, had been an outstanding baseball manager with the Memphis Chicks of the old Southern Association baseball league, and Tommy himself had been one of Wallace Wade's greatest blocking backs at Duke. He believed in preparation and coaching during coaching hours and then forgetting football. He loved to play bridge and chess. He had to play for money, maybe not much, but money. And there was no such thing as a night meeting with Prothro. There was no need for extraneous meetings; everything was covered during working hours. He never believed in large squads. He never worried about numbers. He was more concerned with improving the players he had, and I hope I have adopted this philosophy from him. During my two years at UCLA we had only two quarterbacks, Gary Beban and Norman Dow, and that's all we needed. In those seasons we went 17-3-1 and beat national champion Michigan State in the Rose Bowl after losing to them earlier on the regular schedule.

Our only other loss during '65 was to Tennessee at Knoxville, and that's where Prothro was so upset at the officiating he said he was ashamed to be a Southerner, but I don't think he really meant it. Our tie game was with

Missouri. The next year our only loss was to Washington, 16–3, and that was an interesting story which I will relate later.

I must admit in those days I was a much more free-wheeling coach than I am now. I was described as "imaginative, wide-open," which meant I delighted in off-beat plays, end arounds, sleepers, and other unconventional designs. In retrospect, that was because I had not found an identity as a coach, something to believe in. There is nothing wrong with those plays if they are used in the context of the overall offense, not as an offense in themselves.

I mention that as footnote to the 1965 season.

To begin with, in pre-season planning, we had come up with a gadget offense. Not exactly a gadget, but a headset in the quarterback's helmet. Obviously, this has possibilities. Say a quarterback is moving out on a sprint-out pass and the running lanes are wide open. I, observing from the press box, would yell to Beban, "Run, run." My view was better than his. Or it could be the other way around. It might be, "Pass, pass." No limit to what you can do with high visibility from the press box.

We thought we had the headset offense perfected. And no James Bond movie ever perpetrated more intrigue than in the way we guarded our secret. The headset was in a strongbox, under lock and key, transported by one of the managers on the team who skulked from corner to corner. You would have thought the strong box contained the secrets of the hydrogen bomb.

We had picked the Michigan State opener to spring our

secret weapon and all was rigged up for the communication link to Beban. Of course there was to be a
pre-game test.

So I sat in the press box and yelled instructions to
Beban.

He tapped his helmet. That was the signal that he
could not hear. Something had gone wrong. So the secret
weapon had to be abandoned, at least temporarily. Michigan State beat us, 13–3.

There was always next week and Penn State at University Park.

Once more things were set up. And, eureka, this time
everything was working.

Working too well. We were moving the ball like mad,
but an attendant in the parking lot picked up our fre-
quency and rushed over to report our signal to Penn State
coach Rip Engel. Naturally, we packed up the gadget
in a hurry and hid it out, never to be used again, and after
the game, won by us, 24–22, Engel accused us of un-
ethical conduct. That was debatable. This kind of thing
had been used in the pros before, and I am sure there was
no college regulation on it because it had never come up.

Tommy Prothro did not lie about it. I never knew him
to lie. He said, "We always have communication from the
press box to the field," and that was a nice choice of
words.

Anyway, that was the end of the secret weapon, a $500
piece of equipment.

Well, if we couldn't talk to our quarterback, I figured
we could hide our end, and in the seventh game of the

season we pulled out the old sleeper play against the University of Washington. I told coach Prothro we could score once on the sleeper—you can't use it more than once —and he went along. Because they always went into a defensive huddle, the Huskies were the ideal victims for the sleeper.

When we felt the time opportune in the game, we called it. Washington went into its defensive huddle and we went into our offensive huddle. When the Huskies came out of their huddle, Dick Witcher took off and raced to the sidelines as if a sub had come in for him. But once on the sidelines, he skidded to a screeching halt. The ball was quickly snapped to Beban and he threw to Witcher, who jogged to a touchdown.

It was all perfectly legal, but Washington coach Jim Owens screamed that it was a breach of coaching ethics. A real rhubarb developed after the game, won by us, 28-24. Washington officials said we hid out the player and violated all rules, but we didn't. We had made sure the play was legal before we used it.

In the long run I guess it hurt us. The next year we went up to Washington undefeated and they knocked us off, 16-3, for our only loss. That game also knocked us out of the Rose Bowl. I guess they were out to "win one for the sleeper." Then in 1970, the year before I returned to UCLA as head coach, Washington got Prothro down and beat him, 61-20.

The way I see it, I had to share some of the blame because it was my idea in the first place. The sleeper worked once, but that damned play awakened the Huskies for years. I don't understand it. At Florida we used it for a touchdown against Tulane in 1961, and they weren't bad sports about it. Oh well . . .

You know, people have this image of a coach on the sidelines, as brilliant as Solomon in all his glory, with all the answers. He surveys the struggle, spots weaknesses, makes adjustments, gives inspiring half-time talks, and, presto, his team wins in the fourth quarter because he outcoaches the guy on the other side of the field. Sounds easy, nothing to it.

Let me give you an example of coaching brilliance.

It is the last game of the 1965 season and we are playing Southern Cal, our arch-rival, and we're trailing 16–6 late in the fourth quarter. Gary Beban hits Dick Witcher for a touchdown, we make the 2-point conversion, and suddenly we're back in the game at 16–14. We try an onside kick and recover it just past midfield, and now we've got a chance to win the game.

That is when Rodgers, high in the press box, goes into his act. I call Beban to the phone and say, "Gary, remember that 200 X-Post H pattern we used in the first half? You threw it to Kurt Altenberg and it was intercepted. You should have thrown to Mel Farr, the trailing halfback on the play. Let's run it again, and this time throw it to Farr, okay?"

He says, "Okay, coach."

At last I've got Beban understanding what we want to do.

Dutifully, Beban calls 200 X-Post H, Altenberg goes deep, Farr trails on the play, and Beban hauls off and hits

Altenberg for a touchdown, and we win the ball game and go to the Rose Bowl. That is what a great player can do for an ordinary coach. If Beban had thrown to Farr, as I suggested, we might have gained 5 yards on the play.

There is nothing like great coaching.

We go on to the Rose Bowl and upset Michigan State, 14–12, on Beban's touchdown pass and quarterback sweep, and Prothro is named Coach of The Year, an honor richly deserved.

As I mentioned, Prothro did not believe in large squads. We had two quarterbacks, Beban and Norman Dow, and there came a time in 1966 when we needed Dow. Beban was the complete quarterback, later a Heisman Trophy winner. Dow did not have the natural talent of Beban, but he practiced every day as if he were getting ready for the Rose Bowl.

Going into the SC game of 1966, we found we'd be without Beban, who was hurt, and Prothro gave one of the most inspiring pre-game talks I've ever heard.

He said, "Men, now no disrespect for Noman Dow, Gary Beban is a great football player and he has won a lot of football games for us. On the other hand, no disrespect for Gary Beban, but football is not a one-man game, never has been, never will be. What we're going to have to do to win this football game is to play like Norman Dow has practiced. That means we're going to have to play with great intensity, do all the things we have to do, be ready, do all the things that will win for us."

I'd love to say that Norman Dow dashed out and completed ten passes or ran for a hundred yards. He didn't.

He ran for about twenty yards and passed for about thirty, but we won the game, 14–7, because the rest of the team played like Norman Dow had practiced.

I'll always remember Norman Dow because he meant a lot to me as a football player. He was a symbol of what the game is all about. The most important part of coaching is to develop players to their maximum. Not just the Gary Bebans, but the guys behind the Bebans.

Before the SC game Dow had played ten minutes of football. He wanted to play and his mother and father wanted him to play, and they used to call me and ask why he wasn't playing. The reason he did not play was that Beban was ahead of him. When his opportunity came he took full advantage of it under difficult circumstances, and for that I must admire Norman Dow and all the Norman Dows of football.

Everyone has disappointments in football. I had one in the spring of '66 when I was interviewed for the United States Military Academy head coaching job after the resignation of Paul Dietzel.

My first meeting was encouraging. We talked as if the job was mine and all they needed was a little time to get things in order. I returned to Los Angeles for spring practice and further word from West Point. The call came. They wanted another meeting. That puzzled me.

And Prothro was upset. He got on the phone and spoke to Army officials.

"Listen, we're having spring practice," he said. "Do you want Pepper or not." The Army spokesman said he wanted another meeting. So back to New York I went, and this time the atmosphere has changed radically. They're talking about whether I can adjust to New York. Can I get along with the New York press? Would I be interested in a one-year contract? Something happened. Somebody got to them. Later I learned someone, hearing they were interested in me, called and told them I was too immature. It was not hard to detect that their minds had been changed for them.

When I returned to UCLA, I found someone else's coat in my office and the schedule on the wall had me conducting study hall that afternoon.

I had to laugh.

In a period of twelve hours I had gone from head coach at West Point to study hall teacher.

I consider my two apprentice years at UCLA two of the most important in my development as a coach. I had been exposed to a variety of coaches. Ben Martin at Air Force was low-key, relaxed, not uptight about the score or every play, a man of humor and compassion. Ray Graves at Florida was absorbed in details, whether we should have sausage or bacon for breakfast, a good recruiter and alumni organizer. Tommy Prothro at UCLA was highly organized, a straight shooter who exerted little or no pressure on assistants, not worrying whether he came to work at 10 A.M. or noon if the plans had been formulated.

Chapter IX   *Pop, Probation, and a Twelve-man Defense*

"Let me know in a day or two," I said to Wade Stinson and prepared to leave Lawrence, Kansas, and return to Los Angeles.

"Why don't you just go on out to the motel, stick around for a few hours, and I'll call you," Stinson said.

I had just been before the screening committee at Kansas University which was looking for a head coach to replace Jack Mitchell. I did not apply for the job. Stinson called me for the interview.

So a driver came around in this big car and I was chauffeured back to the motel. An hour or two later the phone rang and it was Stinson.

"The job is yours," he said.

"Fine."

Getting a head coaching job was easier than I expected. I made two trips to West Point and things went from a near handshake to a sudden freeze. Along the way there had been feelers from Brown and Vanderbilt. After nine years of apprenticeship at Air Force, Florida, and

UCLA, I expected to sweat a little before I got a job. The people at Kansas were decisive and I admired them for it. The only other candidates, according to the newspapers, were Don Fambrough, an assistant from the Mitchell staff who stayed on with me, and Bill Pace, then an assistant at Arkansas. From what I understood, Tommy Prothro had recommended me when he spoke at the annual KU banquet earlier that month, and Darrell Mudra, who applied for the job, had also thrown my name into the hopper.

The announcement was made Friday, December 16, 1966. I mention that because it was an interesting day.

Thirty minutes after the press conference in Lawrence, Kansas State announced that Vince Gibson, a thirty-three-year old Alabaman, had been named to succeed Doug Weaver as head coach.

We were not strangers Our careers almost paralleled each other. He played his college football at Florida State about the same time I was at Georgia Tech. He was an assistant coach at Florida State when I was at Florida, and we had recruited against each other. But, as time was to prove, our Florida rivalry was nothing compared to the heat that was to be expended by two Southerners in the Sunflower State.

We made the usual statements to the press.

"We anticipate recruiting all over Kansas and also spreading out," I said.

"We want to keep Kansas kids in Kansas, whether they go to KU or K-State," Gibson said. Suffice it to say, he preferred K-State, and in the next four years our battle lines were drawn over recruiting and it was alley fighting at its best, or worst. We had different styles and I am not saying either one was right or wrong. At Georgia Tech life was not a cutthroat thing. Vince had gone to South Georgia and Florida State where everything was scratch and fight, and he was as successful in his way as I hope I was in mine.

When I left my job at UCLA, I anticipated a friendly round of recruiting. I got my feet wet in a hurry, and the battleground was not the state of Kansas, but, ironically, my old hometown of Atlanta, Georgia, where Kansas and Kansas State met in mortal combat the following May.

My busiest recruiter at the time was my father, Franklin, who was prone to get overzealous in his family loyalty.

Franklin signed three kids from Atlanta, Roy Stanley, Sugar Bear Crawford, and Charles Arline. In his zeal, he neglected to tell us he had obtained the signatures two days before the legal signing date.

Really, this scene was like an old Leon Errol movie, skulking around motels and hiding people out and all that. Unfortunately for Franklin and for us, a Kansas State birddog scout reached Stanley the next day and was told, in all innocence, "Oh, I signed last night."

Aha, the plot thickens, and the scout rubbed his chin and attached his tape recorder to the phone.

"Oh, that's nice, kid," he said. "Now tell me all about it. Did Mr. Rodgers give you any money? Did he hide you out? Give me all the details. Don't leave anything out."

A few days later the tape was in possession of Vince

Gibson, who then called his school president who then called my school president. The Kansas president said he would fight the charge if Franklin hadn't signed the prospects early, and I asked Franklin and he said, "Who, me?" He went out and got affivadits all over the place, but, as the Crime Doctor used to say, he made one mistake. His times marked down for signing Stanley and Crawford were the same and they lived ten miles apart. That detail was only academic because Big Eight commissioner Wayne Duke had the incriminating tape.

Now, big investigation. Duke went everywhere looking for Franklin and everywhere he stopped, Franklin had just left a few minutes earlier. I never knew Franklin was that mobile. He would have made a hell of a CIA agent.

Finally exhausted, Duke came to me and said, "Pepper, we know this happened. If you can get John Cooper to tell the whole story, I don't think the penalty will be that severe." So I went to Cooper, our chief recruiter and a good one, and told him if he wanted to change his story it was okay with me. I'd back him.

Cooper told everything, even about Charles Arline, which Duke didn't know about and, I'm a son of a gun, the Big Eight Conference threw the book at us. They took away fifteen scholarships, banned Cooper from recruiting for a year and placed Franklin, described only as an "unidentified source," on probation. The loss of scholarships has a delayed reaction on a team and after we had gone 5-5 and 9-1 my first two seasons, we tailed off drastically.

That was the beginning of sort of an undeclared war between Kansas and K-State.

We turned them in on Vince O'Neil, who had started out at K-State, transferred to a junior college, and signed with us. The charge was recruiting irregularities, and K-State was put on probation for a year. They, in turn, blew the whistle on us on a boy named Thompson, and we received another reprimand plus the loss of another coach. Everybody was spying on everybody else. It was wild.

Funny, how these things go. You do all this, have all this competition on a professional rivalry, yet you chat and act like nothing has happened when you chance to meet. But Vince Gibson had one habit that grated on my nerves. He called me "Buddy."

Like the time I called a prospect's house and he answered the phone with, "Hello, Buddy."

"I am not your buddy," I said.

He was in the prospect's house and that wasn't good, but that wasn't the reason I blew my top. I detest being called "buddy." Call me Pepper or coach, anything but "buddy." When I was at Kansas and at UCLA, people from the South that I hardly knew would call and say, "Hey, buddy, howya doin'?" If every man is not a brother and every girl not a sister, every acquaintance is not a buddy.

I got even with Gibson. Later, upon obtaining our practice schedule (if that shocks you, we had their practice schedule, too), he called about an item at the bottom that read "run coaches."

"Do you run your coaches?" he asked.

"Run my coaches?" I said. "Everyone runs at Kansas. Our coaches run almost as much as our players. It's good for morale."

I understand that he began to run his coaches, and they were all cursing the day they'd heard of Pepper Rodgers.

We snookered K-State on another deal. Both schools were after a sensational Virginia high school back, and his decision was in doubt right up to the last minute. Then Dick Tomey, one of our coaches, said the kid really admired Gale Sayers, the Kansas immortal, and could we somehow present him with a Sayers award?

"Sure," I said.

I hurried down to a sporting goods store, bought a little trophy about three inches high and then, at the boy's high school assembly, I made the presentation of the "first annual Gale Sayers Scholarship Award."

What happens in Kansas—and in other states—is that the alumni force you to fight over prospects who aren't actually very good. I don't blame Vince Gibson and others. You get caught in quicksand not of your making. Every one, every town has an all-America prospect, and you are afraid you will miss him.

On one nightmarish morning, about 2 A.M., I had just taken a Sominex and was trying to get to sleep when the phone rang. One of our assistants, Charlie McCullers, was calling from Columbus, Kansas, and he said that a prospect, one Rich Jones, would sign if I got there by 8 A.M.

No way I could do that. I was bone-tired.

But Charlie was insistent.

"Vince Gibson told him you won't be here," he said. "Gibson said you didn't think that much of him."

That was it, the magic summons. I called John Novotny and he drove while I slept and we got to Columbus and signed the kid and he never played a down for us. That's what I mean about being caught in outside pressures. You sign a kid to keep him away from another school and then you wish he had gone there.

Our rivalry with K-State spilled over into other areas. You can't afford to overlook anything. We had psychological warfare going on all over the place. Our slogan was "Pepper Power." At Manhattan, Kansas, Gibson was knee deep in "Purple Pride." He had the stadium painted purple. Their uniforms were purple and, I guess, even their hot dogs and beer were purple. They slapped purple paint on everything from toilet seats to fire hydrants. From what I heard, later when Vince went to Louisville, he initiated a "Crimson Pride" campaign.

During my first two years at Kansas "Pepper Power" won out over "Purple Pride." In our first meeting in Lawrence, we won 17–16. The next year, at Manhattan, we won, 38–29. Then, during that third season with our ranks depleted by the loss of those scholarships, K-State came to Lawrence and beat us, 26–22. The only team we beat that year was Syracuse.

In the meantime, anticipating a keen rivalry between the two schools, Governor Bob Docking had announced he would award a cup to each year's winner.

I had this neighbor, Charlie Himmelberg, a Notre Dame graduate, and he wanted to make sure I remembered the game. So at 2 A.M. in the morning there was a knock on my door. And there was Charlie to present me with an award, a purple jockey strap mounted on a plaque. Charlie was the same guy who sneaked around at night and cut large "L's" in my grass every time we lost a game. Since I was not a dedicated yard man, his "L's" were all too obvious to passing motorists and pedestrians.

As a small town, Lawrence had many advantages. People were interested in the football team and they were friendly. That was one of the disadvantages, too friendly. They'd stop you in the supermarket and quiz you on your game plan or want to know why you didn't pass more and why you didn't play so-and-so because he was better than the guy you were playing. Because everyone knows everyone else in a small town, you have to answer more questions than at a big city school, where you are anonymous and college football is not the only game in town.

My first year at Kansas we went 5-5. I always figured it would have been 6-4 if Oklahoma hadn't thrown its "Citrus Offense" at us during a game at Norman. We were leading 10–7 late in the fourth quarter when Sooner fans, looking forward to their trip to the Orange Bowl, started pelting us with oranges. That broke our concentration and they went 99 yards and beat us, 14–10, on a pass from Bobby Warmack to Steve Zable.

Something good always comes out of something bad.

In the midst of the barrage, I noticed our defensive end, Vernon Vanoy, peeling an orange for his daily supplement of vitamin C.

The Sooners beat us again the next year, 27–23, but it

was our only loss and this time we went to the Orange Bowl, and once more I proved that something good can come from something bad.

Before we made the trip to Miami, we steamrolled our way through a high-scoring season—47–7 over Illinois, 38–20 over Indiana, 68–7 over New Mexico, 23–13 over Nebraska, 49–14 over Oklahoma State, 46–25 over Iowa State, 27–14 over Colorado, 38–29 over K-State, and 21–19 over Missouri. This was the first Kansas team that had won as many as nine games in sixty years, and it was the school's first major bowl game in twenty years. Ironically, the only other trip to Miami resulted in a 20–14 loss to my alma mater, Georgia Tech, in 1947.

Our kids—John Riggins, Bobby Douglass, Ron Jessie, John Zook, Karl Salb, Donnie Shanklin, Larry Brown, Jim Bailey, and the others—had had a great year and deserved the invitation to play Penn State on January 1.

As for me, it was a homecoming of sorts, a return to the state where four years earlier, almost to the day, Ray Graves left a piece of yellow legal paper on my desk informing me I was fired. I'd be lying if I said I did not savor the trip back to Florida with my own bowl team.

As things turned out, returning with ole Pepper was that old standby, controversy.

That evening in the Orange Bowl I introduced a revolutionary twist to the game of football, a twelve-man defense in an eleven-man game. Not since Roy Riegals ran the wrong way in the 1929 Rose Bowl had a boner been as widely publicized as ours. We lost the game, 15–14, but how we lost it was the intriguing part.

Now imagine the scene . . .

We're ahead, 14–7, late in the fourth quarter and we have the football on the Penn State 5-yard line. Now, you'd say the game is in a bag. If we kick a field goal, we're ahead 17–7 and the game is safely tucked away. But it is fourth down and 1 yard to go, and I tell Bobby Douglass to give the ball to John Riggins and surely John can get a yard and we'll go in for a touchdown. We give the ball to John and then something unfunny happens. He doesn't get a yard and Penn State takes over on its own 5-yard line and the game is not in the bag, still relatively secure but not in the bag.

We mess around a little bit and get a punt partially blocked and Penn State gets the ball around its 40-yard line with about 90 seconds to play. At that point, I'd take our chances over theirs. Now out of timeouts, Penn State throws a long pass to stop the clock and, lo and behold, their halfback, Bob Campbell, catches it deep in our territory and now I am sending tackles back in to replace the two extra linebackers that we put in for an expected passing blitz. Only one linebacker, Rick Abernathy, is so caught up in the game he doesn't come out. He's wild, he's taking tackles, and he stays in the game for four plays during which Penn State scores.

Now they go for a 2-point conversion on a pass and we knock it down and everyone is jumping up and down and dashing on the field and patting each other on the shoulders and celebrating a 14–13 Kansas win. But wait a minute. There is a flag on the field. An official penalizes us for having too many people on the field and Penn State gets another shot at a 2-point play. They run over a 2-point conversion and win, 15–14, and Rodgers becomes the first coach in history to lose a bowl game because he used twelve players in an eleven-man game.

That makes me a dumb coach. It makes Joe Paterno a brilliant coach.

There he is in the fourth quarter, sixty yards from the goal line with no time outs left, and he tells his quarterback to throw a long incomplete pass to stop the clock. So Bob Campbell jumps up and catches that pass and Penn State has us in trouble. After the game when reporters ask Paterno why he threw that long pass, he says, "We noticed the safety cheating a little."

Heck, I would have said the same thing.

In retrospect, we didn't lose the game on the twelve-man penalty. We lost the game when I called a fullback run on fourth down instead of kicking a field goal, but few remember that part of the game and I'm not one to remind them. In a way, I am glad the game ended the way it did. If it had ended with us leading, 14–13, and films later showed twelve men on the field, then I'd HAVE TO MAKE A DECISION.

Anyway, I'll bet most people who can't name you Orange Bowl scores or games can tell you that Pepper Rodgers lost an Orange Bowl game because he played twelve men.

You know, everything goes well when you're winning. Players are heroes and a coach is a wise old bird. Even losing the Orange Bowl was a conversation piece. Then you start losing for one reason or another, and the climate changes. My third year at Kansas wasn't very successful from a record standpoint, 1-9, and then the rumors started. My players were using drugs. They were drinking and keeping late hours. They had girls in their rooms. They were fighting and brawling. We had too many blacks in one room, too many whites in one room. They were smoking marijuana. I began getting calls at night, so during the week of the next game, I spoke to the squad.

I told them we were getting ready to play a tough game and I didn't want anyone calling me at three o'clock in the morning with complaints about misbehavior or rowdyism.

Sure enough, early the next morning, there was a call that my fullback, John Riggins, was trying to kick down the door to a girl's apartment.

I called in John and asked him about it and he said it was not true and I believed him, but he had been out after curfew and he had been drinking so I suspended him from the squad for the next game. I told him I had given him fair warning and evidently he didn't understand what I was saying, and if he wanted to play by his rules he'd have to get his own team because I had the only team in Lawrence, Kansas. Possessed of great athletic ability and one of three athletic brothers from Centralia, Kansas, Riggins was a bright boy and a free spirit and thus not an easy guy to coach in a small town where people weren't as tolerant as those in big cities. Personally, what he did didn't bother me, but the talk always got back. When you win, everything's fine; when you lose, the guy you had a beer with the other night becomes

9. At this stage of a game there is not much a coach can do except exhort, scream, run in circles, and perhaps slowly go out of his mind.

10. During a Monday practice I am explaining what happened on the previous Saturday to Al Ciraldo, long-time "Voice" of Georgia Tech. Whatever happened must not have been good.

11. In this 1974 photo, Atlanta Mayor, Maynard Jackson (left) offers a few tips before my exhibition match with tennis star Stan Smith (center) in a downtown Atlanta park.

12. As one TV personality to another, I corner Bob Hope at the Atlanta Airport to tape a segment for my first "Pepper Rodgers Show" in 1974.

13. Five giants of the links, Gary Player, Bob Griese, Arnold Palmer, my son Kelly, and me at the Atlanta Golf Classic Pro-Am. It is sort of deflating when a kid standing around asks, "Who's that with Kelly?"

14. The Rodgers and friends Phil Walden of Capricorn Records and Jimmy Carter. The one with the nice smile is Carter. *(Tom Hill Photography; Atlanta, Georgia.)*

15. Pepper and wife: The thing I like about Janet is that she never asks why we don't pass more.

an ass. You lost because you were drinking beer. Because he liked to have a good time, Riggins created problems, but not as many as people would like for you to believe.

John was the highest professional draft choice. (No. 1 by the New York Jets) I ever coached, and a few years later when I was at UCLA a pro scout dropped by and began talking of him. He told me his team did not draft Riggins because of his partying reputation, and I pointed to the practice field where my team was working out.

"See that team out there?" I said. "There's not one guy that I know anything about, where they go, what they do. They might raise hell three times more than John Riggins, but you don't know it because this is a big town. When I was at Georgia Tech, back in the early fifties, players were raising hell and fighting more than they could have possibly done at Kansas, but Atlanta was a big city and players could get lost, and they got away with some things because they were well known. In small towns athletes are judged harshly.

"Just because a guy drinks a little beer and isn't in bed at nine o'clock doesn't make him a bad person. That doesn't necessarily mean I want him to do that, but I don't have my head in the sand. I played with a lot of people at Georgia Tech who didn't put their head in the sand at nine o'clock.

"My idea of disciplining players is the same as Tommy Prothro's. His rule of thumb was to imagine a player had so much money in a bank. When he withdrew all his money, his account was ended."

I still go by that guideline.

The drug scene was active in the late 1960s. I was told a player of mine was selling marijuana in a dormitory. That threw me because I really didn't know that much about drugs. First thing I did was protect myself by calling his parents. I learned that a long time ago. Call the parents. This particular boy was from a prominent family and his mother and father said there was no way their son could be doing something like that. Later he was caught and denied everything. No one is going to admit anything like that.

Another one of my players moved out of an apartment because marijuana was being baked in an oven.

A coach is usually the last to know these things. How do you catch people? You can't run around asking people if they use marijuana. Now that I know more about drugs I am not quite as hung up on the issue, not quite as nervous about them. Until we know something, until we have an experience in our lives, we are really confused. Advice from the outside is cheap. People tell you how you should handle your players, how you should handle your kids. My way is to consider the individual and not make a blanket indictment that everyone is bad, everyone drinks or doesn't drink, smokes or doesn't smoke. I certainly would not throw a first offender off my squad, neither would I keep a habitual rule breaker. I'd like to give everyone a chance to do his or her own thing within the realm of the rules, within the confines of what they have to do.

Coaches are not infallible. I made some mistakes at Kansas. One of them was in moving Donnie Shanklin from halfback to flanker. I reasoned that he wasn't big enough to run and, with Bobby Douglass throwing those darts, he'd be the Jerry LeVias type and catch a ton of passes.

I was positive about that, but I was wrong.

His senior year I moved him back to halfback and he did a fantastic job of running, returning punts, and kicking. He was just a great football player. He wasn't moved because he wasn't good enough or because I wanted to make a wide receiver out of him. He was moved because I made a mistake and I told him so. That is part of growing up as a football coach, understanding you are not infallible and you can make the same mistakes as others.

The Shanklin mistake wasn't my only one. During the summer of '69, following the Orange Bowl game, I was in Atlanta to coach in the Coaches All-American game and stick both feet in my mouth. One reason I quit drinking was because of some of the talk—including my own—that comes out of cocktail parties. I was sitting around drinking and chatting with members of the media, including a writer from *Sports Illustrated*, when I mentioned Missouri had never won the Big Eight championship since Dan Devine had been there. At Kansas, during my first two years, we had had pretty good success against Missouri, winning, 17–6, and, 21–19.

When this story came out in *Sports Illustrated*, it was more like Rodgers saying Devine chokes, he can't win the big one. I learned then that (1) I shouldn't drink or (2) I should drink alone.

We played Missouri in the last game of the 1969 schedule. "Played" is not exactly the word for it. The last time I looked up at the scoreboard the score was 69–21 and Kansas wasn't leading. That afternoon Devine gave us a spectacular, sensational licking.

That's where I picked up one of my banquet-circuit lines. I told people I conceded in the fourth quarter and gave Devine the peace sign, and he returned half of it.

Missouri also beat us in 1970, my last year at Kansas, and Devine and I finished up with 2-2 records. If there is one thing that incident taught me, it is that you don't antagonize people. Devine does win the big games. And he wins some of them BIG.

Boulder, Colorado, is a beautiful city just outside Denver, and some strange things go on there, or went on there. In 1970, two weeks before our Missouri finale, we traveled up to Boulder for a game with the Colorado Buffaloes. It seemed like everyone had it in for ole Rodgers that year. We got waxed, 45–29. It turned out the year 1970 was the year for dirty tricks, and all of them weren't in Washington.

I noticed the Buffaloes were foaming, if not roaming, that day and I soon discovered why. A prediction column out of the Kansas City *Star* had certainly prepared them psychologically. It read: "Another meeting of teams out of the Big Eight title chase. Colorado, which CAN'T WIN the tough ones, figures to be OUT OF GAS after flopping against Oklahoma, Missouri, and Nebraska the last three weeks. Kansas HAS THE MOMENTUM despite last week's loss at Oklahoma State . . . The measuring stick is the seniors and Kansas has the clear edge. For example, at fullback, it's a matchup between the league's best rusher, John Riggins, and JOURNEYMAN, Ward Walsh. The same comparison carries right down the line with 263-pound Steve Lawson CLEARLY BETTER than the Buffaloes' best offensive tackle, Jim Phillips; 284-pound Bob Tyus STRONGER and SUPERIOR to the SLOWISH CU offensive tackles, Rich Variano and Dave Capra, and linebacker, Gary Davenport, HEAD-AND-SHOULDERS above Phil Irwin. KU doesn't have any offensive linemen as good as Don Popplewell and Dennis Havig, but these two won't be enough . . . It will be Kansas 21, Colorado 10."

A writer got hold of the "article" after we lost. Then it was discovered it was a bogus bit of journalism written by an assistant coach at Colorado and printed in the Kansas City *Star* Logo in a Boulder print shop. The genuine Kansas City *Star* prediction column picked Colorado to win by 24–14. No one will know how many of the Colorado players "bought" the phony article. But Don Popplewell should have been suspicious. He was a mail subscriber to the *Star*.

As I always say, never underestimate the power of the "press."

Four years earlier, at Boulder, a low-flying aircraft scattered leaflets downgrading the Buffaloes during the week of the Nebraska game.

Different strokes for different folks. I don't knock these things, but you give me superior players and I'll win every time despite all the psyche jobs.

I enjoy the little intrigues of football. I am serious when I get on that field, just as I was serious when I got in that T-33 jet, but I believe everything else about football should be fun. I hope we're not too callous to remember it's a game.

I had fun at the Air Force Academy, at Florida, at UCLA, and at Kansas, and I tried to make it a fun thing for my coaches and players. Of course, it wasn't a fun time in our country. That was the period of the campus revolts, the black revolution, the dope scene, and general unrest among the youth. But, as they say, there is a time to laugh and a time to cry, and sometimes you can laugh while you're crying. Campus movements come, they intensify, and they fade out and make room for another.

We had a black revolution at Kansas. Everyone had a black revolution, and it was good. It cleared the air.

Leaving my office for practice one afternoon, I was confronted by our black players. They informed me they were boycotting the team until a black song or pompon girl was allowed to join the others. Hell, everything revolves around women. I told them, okay, I'd see them when the protest was resolved.

I stopped by the locker room, and there was Vernon Vanoy getting dressed for practice. He had overslept and just arrived.

"Vernon," I said, "the black players are having a boycott."

He looked up at me.

"Okay, coach," he said.

He took off his shoulder pads and left.

Soon a black pompon girl was added and the boycott ended.

The racial issue could be touchy at times, though, even with innocent intentions. During one of our football banquets, Bobby Douglass, after a few highballs, requested the band play "Dixie" for his Southern coach. There was nothing ulterior in it, but, wouldn't you know it, the request found its way to *Sports Illustrated* and its series on the black revolution. It was listed as an example that some Southern coaches make their black players listen to "Dixie."

To me, football players aren't white or black, they're football players. My job is not to be a crusader and espouse one cause or another. My job is to coach a football team. I don't go around giving the soul handshake because it takes too long and it wears out my hand. I deeply resented the magazine's interpretation on why "Dixie" was played at the KU banquet. It was played because Bobby Douglass requested it, no other reason. And he meant no harm.

Bobby Douglass was one of my favorite people. When I arrived in Lawrence, I was told Douglass had been a flop as a sophomore quarterback, but, after a practice or two, I said, "That's my man." He was a strong runner and a good left-handed passer. If I were taking over a pro team today, he'd be the first player I'd try to sign. I saw where the Chicago Bears let him go, saying he couldn't pass or that he passed too hard. That's a lot of bunk.

Douglass' problems in the pros probably started with me, and not on the football field. In my entire coaching career I have tried to help negotiate only one professional contract—Douglass'.

As a wheeler-dealer, I flopped.

A Canadian League team was interested in Bobby and sent its coach and general manager to Lawrence for negotiations. Old Rodgers created the atmosphere for the summit. I had Doug Weaver stop by the spirits store and buy the convincer, a bottle of Chivas Regal. Then we invited the pro-football people and Bobby to my home for the hard bargaining. One plus was the CFL coach drank. A minus was the general manager did not. Being a positive thinker, I worked on the plus.

As evening dawned into the morning, the coach was making more and more concessions and I was thinking I had negotiated the greatest professional contract since Joe Namath, and Doug Weaver was writing everything down on a yellow legal pad. "Rodgers," I said to myself, "you've got it, man, you're the Great Negotiator."

Everyone was happy when we staggered to bed.

Then came the early morning, a call from the general manager withdrawing all offers and furthermore, he said, the coach was fired.

That was the end of Pepper Rodgers' career as a professional football agent. Douglass signed with the Bears for a contract far inferior to the one I had demanded.

Douglass was an independent sort. In one game, when he had called a play that was verboten, I summoned him forthwith to a conference on the sidelines. I thought it might look a little silly, the 5-10 Rodgers chewing out the 6-4, 220-pound quarterback, so I told Douglass, "Smile, Bobby, I want you to keep smiling so everyone in the stadium will think we're sharing a joke or discussing what a great quarterback you are. That's it, smile. Now . . . if you call another play like that I'm going to kick your ass to Siberia. Keep smiling, that's it. Now, you knucklehead, get back in the game and follow the game plan."

Douglass was just one of some really great players at Kansas.

Defensive end John Zook, who had been a near all-pro end in the NFL for the Atlanta Falcons, before being traded to St. Louis, didn't seem too impressive when assistant coach Jack Green saw him for the first time. Zook was in a wrestling match and Green was not sold on his strength. But later in the season, the week before we were to play Kansas State and its great quarterback, Lynn Dickey, Green changed his mind.

Working on our pass rush for Dickey, we held a little scrimmage indoors with our front four, Zook, Karl Salb, Jim Bailey, and Vernon Vanoy, charging at the passer. Since this was to be a live scrimmage, we held Douglass out of the workout. We didn't want him hurt. I wasn't about to play quarterback with all that beef up there. We nominated Charlie McCullers, one of our assistant coaches. On the first play Zook shot through everyone, picked up McCullers and deposited him against the base-ball backstop, upside down. McCullers was furious. He jumped up, ran over to Zook and said, "Don't you ever turn your back on me, Zook."

John looked at him a minute, then turned his back.

We all laughed it off and later had a few beers. After that, Jack Green was sold.

But you had to watch that John Zook.

He was a big, Lil' Abner type country boy from Larned, Kansas, or Zook, Kansas, or somewhere in between. He loved the outdoors, and after the football season he invited us to hunt quail with him. My feet were about worn out trudging over those hills and valleys until we reached the area we were looking for.

"This is it," Zook said, stopping on a hill. "The birds are down in that thicket. You guys go on down and shoot all you want."

Anticipation took over, and we scurried down the hill and into the thicket. We're going through these thick briar patches and cutting and scratching ourselves and bleeding when we hear these rapid gun shots. There is Zook on the hill killing birds like mad. Then it dawns on me. We're flushing them out and he's having target practice. The big city boys have just been taken by another country slickeroo.

Our defensive linemen were a colorful bunch. Karl Salb, 6-4, 260 pounds, didn't want to play football. He was a shot-putter in track, and he had his eyes on the Olympics. But we prevailed upon him to play football with the stipulation that he could pursue his track career during the spring. We were just thankful for large favors, like a 260-pound defensive tackle, even if he had to miss spring practice.

Terry Donahue, our youngest coach and really a great guy, almost messed up the whole deal during an afternoon practice session when he put Salb through the torture chamber, banging his head into the tackling machine hour after after hour. Utterly exhausted and fed up, Salb walked off the field. He said he was quitting.

It was time for a conference with Mr. Donahue.

I called him aside. I said, "Terry, my boy, let me tell you a little story. When I was an assistant at Florida and Dick Skelly, a big halfback, threatened to quit the team, Ray Graves gave me some advice. He said he could always find a backfield coach, but it was much harder to find a 6-2, 220-pound halfback who could run a ten-flat. Likewise, Terry, I'm telling you I can always find a defensive coach, but it is much harder to find a 6-4, 260-pound tackle. Get the message?"

Terry got the message. Salb returned to the squad. He passed up his senior year to concentrate on the shot and I think he made a mistake. Football was a diversion that kept him from getting stale.

Terry Donahue was one of my favorite people. He later went with me to UCLA and I tried to hire him at Georgia Tech. He is young, enthusiastic, a good sport, and at Kansas I loved to tease him. I got my chance during the morning of The Big Race, a five-mile marathon I ordered for our coaching staff on the first practice day of the 1967 season. There was a method behind the madness. Our players had to run every day, and I wanted our coaches in condition to run with them. If you make it a game, they enjoy it more. Don Fambrough and Doug Weaver, the two elder statesmen on the staff, chose up sides and we were ready for the big event.

Most of our coaches showed up in sweats and old

sneakers, but Terry Donahue came in with all this modern track clothes and spiked shoes. No doubt he was caught up with the Kansas track tradition that has produced such greats as Wes Santee, Glenn Cunningham, and Jim Ryun. Unhappily, Donahue resembled none of them at the finish.

Terry and Dick Tomey, slightly older, ran the last leg of the relay and Donahue had a substantial lead as they disappeared behind the stands on one end of the stadium just before the start of the stretch drive. Those on Terry's team were celebrating and looking forward to bragging rights when to their amazement, coming into sight onto the stretch was Tomey, all by himself. No Donahue. The old warhorse was out front and the young lion was nowhere to be seen.

Tomey crossed the finish line and staggered to a bench, and his wife Mary ran screaming out of the stands and accused me of trying to kill her husband.

As I explained it was all for conditioning and health, I caught a glimpse of Donahue, slowly locomoting from behind the stands and coming in on a heel and a prayer, an exhausted young man. The Great Race was over and we all adjourned for a beer bust.

There was a purpose in the coaches' relay. It involved the coaches in what the players were doing. There was also a purpose in my rock solo before the squad that first summer in Lawrence. We had been having two-a-day practice for a week or so and everyone was leg weary and short-tempered and we needed a change. We hired a rock band and Don Fambrough stood out on the stage and moved his lips as the band vocalist sang behind the curtain.

I excused myself and went outside where I quickly dressed in hippie garb, wig, shades, tattered shirt and pants, the whole schmeer. I knocked on the side door and Fambrough answered.

"Can I see coach Rodgers?" I said.

"I'd like to go out for football," I said and then, strumming my guitar, I sang my own composition . . .

> I wanted to go out for ball,
> 　　But Rodgers he wasn't fair.
> I told him I'd climb, or crawl up the wall,
> 　　But I would not cut my hair.
> He told me it was lots of fun,
> 　　But I would not cut my curls.
> So you keep your jocks and I'll keep my locks,
> 　　And I'll wind up with the girls.

By then they had figured out that their off-key little coach was singing and I received the old Bronx cheer from the players. The show livened things up. Tired players forgot about their aches and pains, at least until the next practice. There is more to football than practice, and if others don't need breaks in the monotony, I do. I need to do the stimulating things that keep me alive.

One of my little practical jokes almost backfired on me. A student newspaper sports writer called to say he wanted to do an in-depth piece on the coaching staff, and

I invited him over. We had it all set up when the writer, a sensitive little guy wearing thick glasses, reported to my office with my pen and clipboard.

As we were chatting and he was taking notes, J. D. Hixon and Charlie McCullers barged out of the next office as if in heated argument.

"I want him on offense," shouted McCullers.

"Ridiculous, he belongs on defense," snapped Hixon.

The eyes of the student reporter got as big as billiard balls.

"What's their problem?" he whispered to me.

I played it cool. "Oh, nothing," I said. "They're fighting over an outstanding sophomore football player."

"They are?"

"Uh, huh."

I turned to Hixon and McCullers.

"Hey, you guys, go on down the hall and settle it," I said.

They pushed each other down the hall. Then we heard the damnedest sound effects, like they were killing each other. They ripped their old T-shirts and poured stage blood all over each other and returned to the room.

The little reporter was writing like mad and I was beginning to get concerned.

"Hey, it was all a practical joke, they were joking," I said.

"You'd better hope I think it's a joke," he said.

He got the last laugh.

I thought we had some accomplishments at Kansas. though my record in four years was 20-22, slightly under

.500, we had a 9-1 season, went to the school's first major bowl game in twenty years, were ranked sixth or seventh in the nation, depending on your preference of wire service polls. In a personal nature, I was named Big Eight Coach of The Year in 1967 and 1968. We went through the black revolution and the campus revolts and came out healthy and well. We developed all-American and pro prospects.

Despite all this, I am remembered as the coach who did cartwheels leading his team on the field, the coach who sang Christmas carols on television, the coach who put on a wig and sang a rock song, the coach who conducted a marathon race for his assistants, and the coach whose father put him on probation.

That's fine with me. You've got to get their attention before you can get their respect.

Chapter X   *I Make it Back to Hollywood,*
                      but Miss Out on the Roses

The phone is the most important instrument in the life of a coach. You can be hired by phone; fired by phone. You talk to prospects and prospects talk to you. You scout and are scouted by phone. Alumni praise and damn you by phone. Often you dread the ringing of the phone; other times you welcome it.

After the 1970 season at Kansas I received a call from my good friend J. D. Morgan, the athletic director at UCLA. He said Tommy Prothro had resigned to accept a challenge in pro football, and it was indeed a challenge to replace the highly successful George Allen of the Los Angeles Rams.

"Would you be interested in the UCLA job?" he asked.

I told him I would. Basically, I am a big city guy. And I cherished my days as an assistant under Prothro.

A few hours later the phone rang again. This time it was Tommy Prothro.

"Pepper, I've always said a man shouldn't take a job where the previous coach had been highly successful," he said. "But I am doing the same thing. I am going in where George Allen has compiled a high percentage winning record. I thought you'd like to know the UCLA job is open."

I told him that J. D. Morgan had called earlier.

I knew the pitfalls of UCLA. It is a great school with strong leaders, both academic and athletic, but was sort of the stepchild in Los Angeles. If you started ranking the athletic attractions in the city, you'd have to start with the Rams, then the Dodgers, then SC football, then UCLA basketball. That meant UCLA football was about fifth. There was a reason. SC had the alumni strength and many of the newspapermen went to school there. If they are biased, it is not because of any maliciousness. It is simply they are alumni of SC. All of these disadvantages are things you can live with. The biggest obstacle of all is that UCLA has no campus or home stadium. Their team must play across town in the Los Angeles Coliseum, which is on the SC campus, and it is most difficult to get students used to making the trip across town for a game. It would be like getting SC to play in Westwood.

I've heard football coaches say they would never take jobs at a school where a coach like John Wooden had been so successful in basketball. As far as I am concerned, that is ridiculous. I had a most compatible relationship with Wooden and I admired him greatly. Fact is, I never missed a home basketball game. Pauley Pavilion was a fun place to take your family or meet friends and spend an evening. There was no problem there. I'd been around successful basketball coaches before, at the Air Force

Academy where Dean Smith was an assistant, at Florida where Norm Sloan was, and at Kansas where Ted Owens put out typically powerful Jayhawk teams. I've never been hung up on rivalry between football and basketball. I'd heard stories that Adolph Rupp ran Bear Bryant out of Kentucky, but I take such talk with a grain of salt.

Weighing all pluses and minuses, I returned to Los Angeles and three of my Kansas coaches, Doug Weaver, Dick Tomey and Terry Donahue, agreed to go with me.

Until our families arrived in Los Angeles, Weaver and I took an apartment in Santa Monica, and compared to us the "Odd Couple" were the Bobbsey twins. Weaver was a neat and orderly person, and as an inveterate newspaper reader who papered the floors with the many gazettes from the Los Angeles area, I drove him nuts.

He said only an earthquake could shake me of the reading habit.

One night as I read and he complained, the house shook and pictures fell off the wall.

"What was that?" Weave asked.

"I think it was an earthquake."

It was. I didn't read again until the next morning.

Everything happened to us, including a robbery that cleaned out our closets when we had a late meeting. We called the police and this bored-looking officer showed up with a clipboard.

"Okay, okay, what happened?" he said with little enthusiasm.

"We've been robbed," I said.

He looked at Weave and then he looked at me and I

could tell there was a dirty and suspicious mind behind those disinterested eyes. He thought he had a couple of real dudes.

"How long you two fellows BEEN LIVING HERE?" he said with a knowing smirk.

After the robbery, we moved to the Bel-Air Sands and decided to cut down on the beer and diet before our wives hit town. I was to cook the first night, Weave the second.

When Weave sat down to dinner, I placed a plate in front of him and tossed a leaf of lettuce on it. Then I dumped two pounds of tuna on the lettuce. He groaned.

The next night he served an eight-pound glob of ground beef, all in one hunk. I groaned.

"Our diet's going great," I said.

"Yea, sure."

Ten minutes later he started on a six-pack of beer.

I was like the nagging wife.

He'd say, "How long before dinner?"

And I'd say, "One minute, don't start on another beer."

About thirty minutes later he'd say, "I thought we were going to eat."

And I'd say, "I didn't want you to get drunk."

To save money, we shared a ride to work in Weave's car, and I infuriated him when I kept switching stations on his radio. "Coach, I don't mind you doing that in your car, but for goodness sake leave my damn radio alone," he would say. "Wouldn't you think I'd have the right to choose my own music in my own car."

That was a most selfish attitude on his part.

Of course there were times when we didn't speak at all during our rides to and from work. Those were the days after Weave's defense gave up too many points to the opponents. I sulked on those days.

At long last, after six months, our families arrived in town and we had one last beer together.

"I want to tell you something before we split up, coach," Weave said.

"Okay, what?"

"Naw, I don't want to tell you."

"Go ahead, tell me."

"All right. Do you know that after every meal I always said, 'Good meal, coach.' You never once said, 'Good job of washing dishes.'"

On that we had another beer.

After two years at UCLA, Doug took a job as head coach and athletic director at Southern Illinois University, and I hired Homer Smith as defensive chief to succeed him.

I needed all the humor I could muster that first year when we went 2-7-1. Tommy Prothro left me a decent team but no quarterback, and my knowledge of the personnel was skimpy. I made a mistake in trying to run a pro offense with a dropback passer and, I did a poor job of making decisions that were my decisions. By that I mean I did well enough on the field, not so well off the field. The only consolation of the season was a 7–7 tie with arch-rival USC.

Two of our finest backs, James McAlister and Kermit Johnson, were lost to us. McAlister was ruled ineligible because there were erasures on his test exam. A leg injury sidelined Johnson for the season.

One thing I learned that first year at UCLA: I am a field coach, not a tower coach. Tommy Prothro had this tower that would rise when you pushed a button and after practice, I would climb aboard and raise it just enough so I could talk to the team.

Well, one day I pushed the button and the damn thing wouldn't stop going up. I was hollering and the team was laughing. Then it got stuck. I was afraid to climb down because it was on an accordionlike support, and I thought it might collapse and crush my hands and feet. The players finally talked me into jumping to the ground. Thereafter, I learned to stay on the ground. No more damn towers for me.

My college coach, Bobby Dodd, was a great tower coach. He used to say that all he did was direct traffic. He'd sit up on that tower with writers and give them angles for stories, but he never missed anything on the field. He'd yell at a back fifty yards away that he was lined up the wrong way. When it was cold, coach Dodd bundled himself up in blankets, and if it was too cold, he'd call off practice and head for his warm office. That was his style. As Bear Bryant said once, "If I coached like Bobby Dodd, I'd get fired."

A coach is a product of all those he has coached for. I picked up some of coach Dodd's methods. But towers are not for me. I want to be on the ground where the action is. I might miss something.

So my first season at UCLA was a disaster. Mistakes, no quarterback, and a tower that didn't like coaches.

In 1972, my second year at UCLA and my sixth as a head coach, an identity crisis was resolved. I found something to believe in, the wishbone offense, and from that point everything revolved around it. I didn't abandon my off-beat plays of the past—the end around, the pass on third-and-one, etc.—they just became a part of the whole instead of an offense within themselves. So-called trick plays belong in football, but in context. To run the wishbone, I selected Mark Harmon, a junior college transfer and son of the all-time Michigan star Tom Harmon. Physically, he might not have been the best football player in the world, but he got more out of his ability than any player I've ever coached.

It was so easy for Mark not to play football. He came from good family, his father a Michigan immortal and sportscaster of our televised games, his mother, the former actress Elyse Knox, his brother-in-law, Rick Nelson. Yet, Mark Harmon was one of the hardest working football players I've ever coached. He was out every afternoon sweating and suffering to perfect what he did, and what he did was run the wishbone. That year we signed a freshman by the name of John Sciarra and he, too, was to be heard from.

We had a "soft-touch" as an opener in 1972, only national championship Nebraska, which had gone thirty-two games without a defeat—or, since my 1968 Kansas team beat them. As we were putting in a new offense and we hadn't seen Nebraska in a year or so, Cornhusker coach, Bob Devaney, and I agreed during the summer to exchange scrimmage films.

This courtesy never materialized. We spotted a fellow with Nebraska connections at one of our practices, and I called Devaney and complained. He denied the guy had official sanction and said if he was spying, he was doing strictly on his own. I believed Devaney, whom I consider a gentleman and a class guy, but, nonetheless, our film exchange deal was canceled.

I have one game football in my trophy room. It is the ball from that 1972 UCLA-Nebraska game played in the Los Angeles Coliseum. In looking back, I'd have to say that was my greatest victory. Efren Herrera kicked a field goal with 17 seconds left on the clock and we won, 20–17.

If we had exchanged films, Nebraska might have beaten us. Who knows? Our offense was more foreign to them than theirs was to us.

In 1972 we lost only three games, to Michigan, Washington, and USC. Along the way we scored 351 points, 38 on Pittsburgh, 65 on Oregon, 42 on Arizona, 37 on Oregon State, 49 on California, 35 on Washington State, and 21 on Washington. We managed only seven on USC and lost, 24–7. Our 8-3 record was good enough for second place in the Pacific-8 Conference.

Individually, we had four backs who rushed for more than 500 yards. Kermit Johnson, who missed the '71 season with an injury, compiled 989 yards for a 7-yard average, James McAlister had 825, Harmon 521, and Rob Scribner 511. McAlister scored 9 touchdowns, and Johnson and Harmon 7 each. The wishbone returned 4,032 rushing yards. That tended to reinforce my belief in that offense in a conference that relied mainly on the I-formation.

Record-wise, the 1973 season was a huge success. We went 9-2, but unfortunately, we lost our opener at Lincoln, where Nebraska blew us out, 42–19, and our closing game to USC, 24–13, when we ran all over the Coliseum grass, punted only once, but committed six fatal turnovers. We broke every rushing record in the land, ran for 612 yards against Stanford, and generally gained at will. If anything exceeded our rushing yardage, it was the controversy. And it started after the Nebraska game.

When you lose as we did at Lincoln, you re-evaluate. We had a coaches' staff meeting and I threw out the question. "Men," I said, "if your jobs depended on the next game, who would you start at quarterback?"

The answer was unanimous: John Sciarra. So Sciarra, a sophomore, became our quarterback until he was hurt in the fourth or fifth game.

Let me tell you one thing, the players are not going to take the blame. They're going to blame the coaches. When we returned from Lincoln, here they came, mostly seniors, lined up outside my office. We worked too hard for the game. We didn't call the right plays. We didn't eat the right food. We didn't do this, we didn't do that. I called a squad meeting and told everyone, "Look, you're not going to blame the coaches and the coaches are not going to blame you. Individually, we'll all accept the blame; collectively, I'll take the responsibility."

Cal Peterson, who later signed with the Dallas Cowboys, said that we worked too hard, and I pulled out the practice schedule from the previous year and showed him it was exactly the same.

There has been a clashing of views on whether spring practice is worth the effort. I can tell you it is. As evidence I offer James McAlister.

In '72 he had played halfback. The next year we moved him to fullback, and that's where he played in the disaster at Lincoln. After the game, I got calls from all over the country telling me my fullback lined up too close to the line of scrimmage. I checked the films and sure enough James was too close, and by being too close, he forced our halfbacks too close and we had a faulty alignment.

This is not to blame James. He had other things on his mind like track. He was a fantastic long jumper and he had his eye on the Olympics, and so during spring practice we never knew from day to day when he would be with us. In the spring a man gets more attention for long jumping 27 feet than he does for making a long practice run. James always wanted to be like O. J. Simpson, and I think he resented the fact that in the wishbone there were other people carrying the football. He might have been the greatest I-back of all time—I really don't know that—but I do know that Kermit Johnson made all-America playing halfback for me at UCLA, I know that John Sciarra was a candidate for the Heisman Trophy, and I know that Rob Scribner averaged 8 yards per run and made the Rams' squad as a free agent.

As a great athlete, James assumed he could play football without the proper practice. And, later into the season when he got more practice, he started to come on, and he had a great first half against Stanford before he hurt a knee and had to be carried off the field. He had never been hurt before, and for a track man, this was a traumatic experience.

In his absence we played Charlie Schumann, and he did some great things for us. The week before the USC game McAlister was back and the whole world was excited about a 6-1, 205-pound athlete who could run a 9.6 hundred and long jump 27 feet.

That week he brought in some white shoes and said he wanted to wear them. I told him I couldn't let him wear white shoes unless he could get some for the entire team. Big surprise, he outfitted the whole team and we played Southern Cal on national TV and lost the game wearing white shoes. Running the football has nothing to do with white shoes unless players are looking at their feet instead of the sidelines.

I'm convinced we made a mistake playing McAlister as extensively as we did in the USC game simply because his lack of timing and practice interrupted the continuity of our offense. It was my decision. Homer Smith wanted to play Schumann. I was wrong. In no way is this a reflection on James' ability. I consider him one of the greatest athletes of all time, but without practice no one is a good football player. No matter what anyone says, practice is important.

James still likes to talk of the wishbone and how it set him back. Football is a game where if one man becomes a star, the rest of the players become his dupes. That's why I like the wishbone. It's an offense that does not depend on one man. It is the complete team offense.

Okay, that was only one of the controversial plots. So far Harmon and Sciarra had just about split the season at quarterback, but now just before the USC game, Sciarra was well and we decided to play him. We considered him the finest wishbone quarterback in the country.

With Mark's father doing the telecast of the game, this created a most sensitive situation. Parents have a tough time understanding things, and that means all parents. I remember one quarterback's father called me at 2 A.M. and demanded to know why his son wasn't playing. I said, "I know how you feel. My son sits on the bench in Little League football and his coach is a dumb-dumb, but I wouldn't call him at 2 A.M. and tell him." So, I'm sure I would have felt the same way Tom Harmon felt, and there was as much pressure on him telecasting the game as on me coaching.

Later, from what I understand, Mark was quoted as saying we did well when the coaches didn't call plays. The coaches always called the plays, and I've called plays from Larry Libertore of Florida to Danny Myers of Georgia Tech.

Okay, we lost to USC and after the game it all started again. Pepper Rodgers can't beat USC, Pepper Rodgers can't beat John McKay. UCLA was favored over USC for the first time in twenty years, and Rodgers blew it. I beat Bob Devaney three out of five, and he's a pretty fair coach and no one mentions that.

But now the wolves were out and they were saying . . .

—"UCLA wonder coach makes one wonder."

—"Why didn't he pass more?"

People always say I had this complex about USC and McKay. That's not true. Oh, we'd take pot shots at each other in the press, but that's normal for two strong rivals. He'd say things about me in a subtle way, and I'd say things about him.

I had some fun when members of McKay's television crew asked me to say something on a segment of his program, a surprise to him since he didn't know about it, and John McKay didn't like surprises.

I said: "John, I've gone out and gotten some big backs, just like you; John, I've gone out and gotten some 270-pound linemen, just like you; John, I've even gotten a few gray hairs, just like you; so, please, John, won't you let me go to the Rose Bowl, just like you?"

He got a kick out of it.

The UCLA-USC game, as an old traditional rivalry, is a most serious game on the West Coast, but as I said earlier, I don't take myself too seriously.

Like before the '73 game, a reporter came up to me and said, "Pepper, I'm doing an inside piece on the game. I want you to tell me exactly what you're going to tell your UCLA team before you take the field against USC Saturday."

I assumed my scholarly somber look and cocked an eyebrow. He tightened his grip on the pen.

"This is what I'm going to tell them," I said in my best doomsday voice.

I pointed to the Trojans' mascot.

"I'm going to tell them to look out for that goddam horse. He'll stomp right over them."

The beginning of wisdom in coaching is when you learn you can't please everyone. When McAlister was ineligible in 1971, Ted Bear, a geologist who helped get him to UCLA, became anti-Pepper Rodgers. I never did understand that. Maybe I was a poor coach, but I had nothing to do with playing or not playing. Maybe he thought I should have sued or something. I don't have that kind of money. I am not Bear Bryant.

As for resolving differences, I prefer to think of the Efren Herrera case. The moment I walked on the UCLA campus I knew I had something special in Herrera, an extremely accurate soccer-style place-kicker. Before I was to leave UCLA, he would win big games for me. Also he would cause me a lot of grief and, later, satisfaction in the manner in which we resolved our relationship.

A few years ago a National Football League lineman—Alex Karras, I think—said he had an intrinsic dislike for place-kickers. The way he put it, they stand around and never get their uniforms dirty and then jog on the field and decide games.

I would assume this statement was made with tongue in cheek, but there is an element of truth in it. What concerns me is the separation between the regular players and kickers. Because of this, I prefer kickers who also play other positions. Then they are "in" the game; part of the team.

Which brings us back to the saga of Efren Herrera.

Efren established his name among the UCLA heroes in 1972 when his field goal beat Nebraska, the defending national champion. He won other games, but in 1973, when we led the nation in scoring and in total offense, our relationship deteriorated. Efren wanted to kick field goals—he had a personal thing going with this Garcia kid at Stanford—and we didn't need field goals. When you are leading by four or five touchdowns, you don't kick a field goal. I had trouble getting this across to Efren.

But, let me start at the beginning.

We were playing the University of Oregon in 1972 and leading, 65–20, and Efren tried one of his patented onside kicks. His talent was so developed he could top a football, run down the field, and recover it himself. On this play he hit his onside kick, ran down the field, and got it himself. Then, realizing what he had done, he slapped the ball with his hand and Oregon recovered it.

I was furious. I called Efren to me on the sidelines and informed him you don't humiliate a team that is trailing by 45 points.

"You embarrassed me, Efren," I said to him. "That was a terrible thing to do. When this game is over, I want you to go over to the coach on the other side of the field and apologize. Tell him it was an error on your part. I distinctly told you to kick the ball long. What you did is an insult to their players."

Having said my piece, I thought the matter was settled. But, lo and behold, I got up the next morning and read the newspapers and Efren was quoted as saying he apologized for the kick but the head coach, Pepper Rodgers, had ordered him to make such an onside kick. And, naturally, the Oregon coach, who later lost his job, used this insulting incident to take the heat off himself.

Okay, that was 1972. The next year when we were the leading offensive team in the country, with fast backs and big linemen, and Efren was the leading place-kicker in the land, we played Stanford and his personal adversary, Garcia. We rushed for 612 yards and won, 59–13, but Efren was unhappy because Garcia kicked two or three field goals.

Then we played Washington State in a tough game at Seattle and we were leading, 24–14, in the fourth quarter with possession at their 25-yard line, fourth-and-one. Now, if there is one thing I learned from coach Dodd, it's you don't go for a field goal in this situation. There is a chance they will block it, execute an onside kick, and win the ball game, even though there is little more than a minute remaining in the game. So we ran an off-tackle play, and they stopped us short. Now they couldn't score two touchdowns from their 25 with less than a minute left.

But Efren was livid with rage. He threw his helmet to the ground and sulked. I didn't know about this until later.

From this game, we moved on to the University of Washington game, next to the last week of the season, and we won, 62–19. I went home with visions of reading the rave notices in the Sunday morning papers. After all, that was the worst licking Washington had ever absorbed, and we were the highest-scoring team in America.

But that wasn't what I read in the Sunday morning papers. Instead there was a headline reading: "Herrera Says He Missed Extra Point on Purpose." He went on to tell reporters he deliberately missed the last extra point because I did not have any feelings for him, the coaches did not have any feelings for him, and we ran regular running and passing plays instead of attempting fields goals on fourth downs deep in opponents' territory.

I could not believe my eyes.

The normal reaction in such a predicament would be to call in Efren, say I did not need him anymore, and dismiss him from the squad for a flagrant breach of ethics. But this concerned me. A Mexican-American, he had not been in this country long, there was a definite language barrier, and Efren felt isolated from the team. Because of the difficulty in communicating, he had trouble relating to the coaches and the others players.

Then, too, Efren Herrera had been a valuable member of our team. His field goal had beaten Nebraska. He had won other games. Only when he began thinking of his personal goals did the trouble begin.

So I called him in for a conference.

"Efren," I said to him, "the idea in the game of football is to score. We can score touchdowns, we've scored a lot of touchdowns, and we can even score two-point conversions after touchdowns, and so we haven't needed field goals. If you think that place-kicking is a one-man operation, if you think you are kicking the ball by yourself, I am going to let you snap the ball, then hold the ball while 250-pound linemen bear down on you, then play right tackle and block, then play the up-back position and pick up those defensive players barreling through there. When you do all these things, you will know that you are not the only person involved in the kicking game. It is a team thing. Your teammates are as much involved as you are.

"You say you feel you are not on the team. Well, it takes a team to kick an extra point or a field goal. What you consider personal goals should really be team goals."

Following our meeting, I talked with our seniors, and they met with Efren, and after three days, I let him return to the squad. He had his personal problems, but we all have them. He was wrong in what he did, and a lot of coaches would have said he was through forever. After all, he had missed an extra point on purpose, and such an admission left him open for later harassment from the stands.

"Efren, what if you miss an extra point next week," I said to him. "Do you know what the fans will say?

"And suppose I put you in on the last play of the game with Southern Cal next week, how do I know you won't be pouting?"

You know what? The next Saturday he missed his first extra point. But that always happens when a player is under stress and pressure. When I was an assistant at the University of Florida, our fullback, Jon McBeth, said he was approached by some unsavory characters to alter the outcome of our game with Florida State. This story broke before the game. So what happened during the game? McBeth fumbled. It almost always happens that way.

Anyway, I thought Efren Herrera deserved a second chance, just as Bobby Dodd had given me a second chance at Georgia Tech. For a while the pros were down on him, but I explained to them he was a tough guy who'd make tackles on kickoffs and he was a really outstanding place-kicker.

It was simply a lack of communications, largely because of a language barrier.

In reinstating Herrera, I told him, "When I look around for you, you'd better be there, and I'd better not hear of you throwing any helmets on the ground."

There were no more problems with Efren Herrera.

And I am proud that my handling of the Herrera case is now part of the sports psychology classes at UCLA. Instead of copping out, I think we salvaged a great little kid . . . and that's what life is all about.

Football is a game of tears and laughs. As the songwriter put it, no one ever promised us a rose garden.

When you deal with human beings, you have tears. You also have laughs, and I thoroughly enjoyed my days in Los Angeles.

Unlike some coaches, I even enjoy the game of recruiting. You win some, you lose some. I recall one that we won at UCLA, but it really wasn't because of our Recruiting Game Plan.

Terry Donahue and I had gone to San Diego to recruit Wally Henry, whose coach was a former all-pro-type defensive player, Earl Faison.

"I'll tell you what we'll do," I said to Terry. "We'll ad-

journ to a bar and pour a few drinks into Big Earl, and
then he'll come around and convince Wally he should
play for us."

Terry was a little dubious.

Anyway, we met Earl and we found us a lounge in the
San Diego area, and we sat there and began drinking.
Terry and I drank beer, and Big Earl was on the heavy-
weight highballs.

After a few drinks, I turned and winked at Terry and
said. "He's about ready."

Big Earl was still going strong.

After another beer, I looked at Terry's half-closed eyes
and said, "Got 'em, got 'em."

Big Earl was talking away and telling us how he used
to kill 'em in pro ball.

Thirty minutes later I was slurring my words. Next
thing I recall was being tapped on the shoulder by Big
Earl, and I lifted my head off the table. Terry and I had
both passed out.

"Time to go," Big Earl says.

He helped both of us out of there.

That's another reason I quit drinking.

Oh yes, Wally Henry came to UCLA, and he caught a
touchdown pass in the 1976 Rose Bowl victory over Ohio
State.

In December 1973 the telephone rang again. As Bear
Bryant would say, it was "Mama" calling from Atlanta.

Chapter XI   *Kids—and Their Parents—Say*
              the Strangest Things

This is a weapon that strikes fear in the heart of every football coach.

The postcard.

The ordinary postcard.

More specifically, the postcard that arrives the day of the game or just before kickoff and is designed to (1) help, (2) sabotage, or (3) confuse.

If you want to drive a football coach up the wall, send him a postcard and mail it on Thursday.

I know about postcards. I've mailed a few. And received a few.

The postcard warfare was introduced to me early in my career when, as an assistant at Florida, I received a message informing me that Georgia Tech was practicing blocking punts.

Egads, here it was mid-week and Rodgers had not considered that possibility. That kind of information—or misinformation—can keep a coach up all night trying to decide whether it is legitimate, whether in fact a Florida supporter has gained access to the Georgia Tech practice, or whether it is a psychological ploy intended to confuse. Coaches have been known to unload their players in a stadium parking lot prior to a game and work on late information received on a postcard.

Deciding to strike back and fight fire with fire, I sat down and wrote a postcard of my own to the Georgia Tech coaches.

On it I scribbled, "Florida has been working on a pass from punt formation."

Now if Tech took its card as seriously as I took mine, their plan to block a punt would be foiled. There is no way to concentrate on blocking a punt when the threat of a pass is there. The first time we moved back in punt formation I discovered that my message had been duly received. A Tech linebacker shouted to his teammates, "Watch for the pass, watch for the pass." We didn't pass, but we did punt without a great deal of pressure.

This kind of psychological warfare goes on all the time in college football. Actually, most sports are built around deception. Baseball pitchers hint they might be throwing a spitball, not that they are, but the mere threat of it presents a mental hazard for hitters. Tennis players rely on psyche jobs and gamesmanship.

Sometimes it doesn't work when the other coach is too honest. For example, when at Florida, I dropped an anonymous postcard to my former co-worker, Jack Green, then at Vanderbilt, informing him we had been working on a lateral from our kickoff return. I failed to count on the basic integrity of Green.

Before the game, he approached Florida head coach Ray Graves and spilled the beans.

I couldn't believe Green.

"Hey, Ray," he said to Graves. "Just wanted you to know that I received an anonymous postcard from Gainesville indicating you would throw a lateral on the kickoff return. I disregarded it and didn't tell my team because I consider it underhanded."

It was news to Graves who was not in on the deception. Green's honesty made me feel like a heel. But, on further thought, perhaps he was using a psyche job of his own, letting Graves know he knew about the lateral and leaving some doubt as to whether he really told his team. If Florida had planned to use a lateral, it was neutralized by Green's confession. See, you start getting suspicious about everything in football.

The late Herman Hickman used to cite a classic of postal disaster.

As line coach at North Carolina State he was concerned about the indifference of his players before a traditional game, so he motored over to Wake Forest and mailed an anonymous postcard to his troops.

He wrote: "You dumb-dumbs, we're going to tear you limb from limb Saturday. Signed—Wake Forest players."

"You know what happened?" Hickman used to say. "Wake Forest came over Saturday and tore us limb from limb. My players were so scared they were running back and forth to the bathroom. I had managed to convince them they were inferior."

That is the way the postcard works. It is the pre-game

tactic. After the game, I always preferred the telephone to harass a rival coach. The telephone is especially effective after you've won a big game.

At Kansas, after we'd beaten Kansas State, we had this guy call K-State coach Vince Gibson and pretend he was a prominent alumnus of that school. The conversation went something like this:

Fake Alumnus: "I've been out of the country, just returned. How much did we beat Kansas by?"

Coach: "We didn't beat Kansas."

Fake Alumnus: "We didn't? What was the score?"

Coach: "Errrr, 54–6."

Fake Alumnus: "WHAT! Why Kansas couldn't beat a girls' school."

After a while, the coach recognizes the fraudulent alumnus, but not before a few gray hairs.

Coaching a football team draws a strong response from the letter-writing public, and as an outspoken and visible coach, I guess I draw a stronger response than most. Some are complimentary, some offering helpful hints, some opposing my life style and utterances on television. Few are neutral, and candidly, I prefer a negative response to no response at all. I try to answer all mail, even those volunteering to coach my Georgia Tech team for me.

Consider this one . . .

Dear Pepper:
Congratulations on the very splendid offensive show against South Carolina.
However, there are three areas in which we fans in my section find glaring need for change and improvement.

(1) Kicking off diagonally is no good. You are giving your opponents the ball on the thirty-yard line without a runback. As soon as they catch on and set up a runback, we are going to look awfully foolish. Surely there is nothing to recommend those diagonal short kicks.

(2) Pass defense is no good. In both the Notre Dame and South Carolina games your defensive backs stood idly as if deliberately letting the receivers be open to catch the ball, then tackled them. I know that is better than allowing a touchdown, and I know that in one-on-one situations it may be necessary. But several times, as many as three or four Tech defenders were within range to bat passes down or intercept them, but they made no move whatsoever. As soon as opposing teams see what is happening, they are going to riddle Tech with completed passes.

(3) Get the plays to the quarterback sooner. You are in danger of delay of game on almost every offensive play because of slow messages to the quarterback, and the boys have almost no time to think what their assignments are in the few seconds between receiving the message and snapping the ball.

I know you appreciate all this free advice on how to coach from a guy like me who has never been on a football field in his life, but these observations seem very glaring from the stands.

Good luck,

Dr. B.

My answer:

Dear Dr. B.:

Congratulations on your splendid office! However, there are three areas we patients in our neighborhood find glaring need for change and improvement:

(1) It would be much better if you would warm your stethoscope before placing it to someone's chest. You are giving your opponents too much advantage by not following what they do.

(2) I wish you would get better looking nurses, as your competition has you out-classed! Your nurses seem to stand around and do nothing.

(3) When you examine the throat, I wish you would not jam the stick down too far . . . and please get it out sooner. I know you appreciate all this free advice on how to be a successful doctor from a guy like me who has never been to medical school in his life, but these observations seem very glaring after watching the way Marcus Welby does it.

Good luck,

Dr. Pepper

And then there is the orderly advice from a faithful alumnus, such as:

Dear Coach Rodgers:

Just a note to say I'm proud of you and Georgia Tech and your 1975 efforts. Let me offer this advice (it's free).

Advice: Discontinue the no-huddle offense.

Reason: (1) It lost you the South Carolina game because the end who should have caught the game-saving TD pass missed his signals and went down the field and blocked instead. (2) It lost you the Auburn game because a lineman missed his signal and caused the game-winning TD to be called back.

Conclusion: Any other advantages of the no-huddle offense are not worth the two lost games.

Best wishes,

I.E. '60

My answer:

Dear Coach I.E. '60:
Just a note to say I'm proud of your support and enthusiasm. Here's an answer to your letter; it's free advice!
(1) Don't write letters of criticism until you know what you are talking about. We did not use the no-huddle offense in the South Carolina game at any time.
(2) In the Auburn game we were not using the no-huddle offense when we had a lineman downfield.
Conclusion: Last year we lost to Auburn using the huddle and this year we lost to Auburn without the huddle. Now . . .

Sincerely

Pepper Rodgers

One of the proudest letters I received came after I decided to leave UCLA for Georgia Tech. I treasure it because it reflects the way a person can change in his thinking. It goes . . .

Dear Mr. Plain,

Since early last December I have thought that I would never write to you again, but as football season approaches I find myself mellowing and now I feel I must write this one last letter. Although I have not yet fully recovered from your desertion and betrayal (as I think of it), I am prepared to let bygones be bygones.
I shall never forget that moment when, at whichever was the first 1972 game after the Arizona game, my roommate and I were sitting in the stands at The Coliseum and watching with mild disfavor the figure of our head coach cross the field. As we animadverted upon your

taste in clothes (you were wearing some blah ochre outfit), I referred to you sarcastically as "Big Bland," whereupon my roommate, spurred by inspiration and the memory of a certain hamburger commercial, changed it to "Big Plain." A legend was born. Somehow in that instant we suffered a revelation and began to see behind your rather nondescript figure a being of almost Olympian joviality and refreshing casualness. Believe me, we appreciated your bringing to UCLA football the attitude that winning, while highly desirable, is not quite as important as having a good time and creating good feelings on the field. Need I say we also enjoyed our composing our encouraging letters to you.

When I heard the news of your resignation I was trying to simultaneously study for my first law exam and watch the news. At the fatal words I sat up and with a cry of rage flung my 1,000 page criminal law book at the television. I am afraid our new coach shows signs of being from the iron-jawed school of football from which you were such a pleasant change. At any rate, I wish you all the best and much success down there in Georgia. One thing, however, Big Plain: If you ever use the 4-Q play to beat UCLA, I'll strangle you.

Best wishes,

Convert Fan

Letters from old high school teammates and/or opponents always ring a nostalgic bell. The following was especially enjoyable because of its cleverness:

Dear Coach (?), Cocky or Lucky, whichever applies to you now:

We on the South All-Star team thought you were lucky,

knew you were cocky, but never dreamed you'd be called "coach."

By way of introduction, my name is Billy Reagin. I made Tom Dempsey famous by inventing the shoe he kicks 63-yard field goals with. At the time of the All-Star game all I could do was skull the newspaper cameraman and next day The Constitution comes out with this story on the one-foot wonder from Savannah Commercial. If you don't remember, it's probably because I was playing behind Sonny George. The few plays I got in on offense, Bill Brigman (remember him?), Lee Owens and Hillman Rhodes were in there with me and I never got to touch the leather. But I did get a 15-yard penalty for holding you Yankees' right end. (We had poor officiating even then.)

And if you see Ed (Bulldog) Carithers you can tell him I think he is the meanest (I don't mean tough, good, etc.) man I ever saw. Y'all punted to us and I laid a damned good knee high block on that squat outhouse and he grabbed me by the neck and knees and wound me once around his neck and threw me like a shot put.

Anyway, I wanted to recommend a local high school player for your Georgia Tech team. His father played basketball against you. You remember him. He's the one who called you "slobbermouth" . . .

Thanks,

B. Reagin

More than anything else, I guess, I get a kick out of letters written by kids. As I believe children have to be taught biases and hatreds, their letters are most revealing not about them, but about their parents. The following letters came from a fourth-grade class:

Dear Pepper,

I am very sorry you didn't win when Georgia played you. They were probably to (*sic*) excited. My teacher almost died. She always talks about you. You really should meet her.

Yours truly,
Billy

Dear Pepper Rodgers,

My teacher and I love you. (Not you, your team!) Half the class does not like your team, so we always have fights.

Your fan,

Bobby

Dear Pepper,

How have you been? I have been fine. I am a big fan for you Pepper . . .

Love,

Diane

Dear Pepper,

I have not been to one of your games so please send five tickets to 2479 Peachtree St., Atlanta, 30309 . . .

Your fan,

Charles

Dear Pepper,

I really like your football team very much. I like number 1 very much. I like number 10 too. I think your whole team is good. Good luck.

James

Those were from the white hats. Now for the other kind . . .

Dear Pepper,

I am not a fan of yours but my teacher is. That is who made me wright (*sic*) you. But I would have anyway . . . My father is for Tech. But I'm not. I'm for Georgia Bulldogs.

Sincerely,

Helen

P. S. Boo!

Dear Pepper,

My teacher made me write to you! I'm a real Georgia fan. Vince is my hero. I'm not one bit sorry that Georgia beat you. Vince Doole (*sic*) is one of the best coaches in the world. You stink! You are a bad loser because you say too many bad words and that's not all you do when you lose. I have only one good thing to say about you. You let your team lose the game to Georgia.

Your enimy (*sic*),

Alyss

Dear Pepper,

My teacher loves Tech but I hate you. I am for Georgia! Your team wasn't in a bowl this year. All of my friends are for Georgia but my teacher. Why do they call you Pepper? I like Tech a little bit. Would you send me an autographed picture?

> Love,
>
> Sally

Dear Pepper,

Where is the world did you get that name? My name is Lucy and I despise you. I'm so glad Georgia beat your terrible team and they were in a bowl and your terrible team wasn't, but that's life, squirt. The only thing nice I have to say about you is I like your hat which you wear all the time. Well I could say bad things about you all day that I shouldn't, but I don't like to waste time with people I hate. Oh, and you are a little to (*sic*) short. Goodbye, ugly.

> Ha, ha, ha,
>
> Lucy

Dear Peppery,

You have a crummy team 'cause you are the coach. I like Mississippi St. and Ga. better.

> Your enamey (*sic*),
>
> Fred

Dear Coach,

I don't really like Georgia Tech. I am for Georgia Bulldogs! Yeah! The only thing I really like is your hat . . . I
don't want you to go to any trouble but all my school-
mates have been asking for an autographed picture of
you so I kind of want one too.

Your hat lover,

Lindy

During all my years as a coach, no mail response was as
great as the one following Georgia Tech's 1975 game with
Georgia when, having agreed to open the dressing room
to the national television camera at halftime, I was faced
with the most difficult chore of talking to a team that was
behind 28–0.

Here were some of the postal reactions . . .

Dear Coach Rodgers,

As I sit here suffering with you Thanksgiving evening,
I can't help but remember an article I read several years
ago. The message of this article was that certain types of
football conditioning programs designed to put on weight
and build strength had the undesirable side effect of making players more susceptible to leg injuries. Could such a
program be the cause of some of our bad luck this year?

Sincerely,

I. E. '62

Dear Coach,

As a UCLA alumn, I was rooting for the Yellow Jackets tonight, but Lady Luck wasn't being much of a lady for you. I admired your team's tenacity to scrap back and perform admirably under the cirumstances.

I was moved greatly by the scene at halftime in your locker room. I am honored to have attended UCLA during your term there . . .

Sincerely,

UCLA alumnus

Dear Pepper,

Just a short note to let you know I enjoyed your "Win One for Pepper" halftime oratory last evening. I surely don't envy you coaches when things go wrong as they did for you in the first half . . .

Sincerely,

Colonel, Air Force Academy

Dear Mr. Rodgers,

I watched the Georgia vs. Georgia Tech game on television and was deeply moved as I am sure many other Americans were by your statement at halftime. The concept that it was the most important thing to try and not to give up has been sadly lacking in both college and professional sports. The emphasis has been in winning and money . . .

Yours truly,

New York Attorney

Dear Coach Rodgers,

I was watching the game against Georgia and I heard the remarks you made about not giving up. I really liked the way you talked and I wouldn't mind playing football for you. I am a junior, 16 years old, 6–3, 175, have a B average . . . and I love to hit.

Yours truly,

Alabama High Schooler

But all letters are not ego-building, as evidenced by:

Being the "nut" I am for the Jackets, why is it so easy to dislike the "loudmouth" coach?

No Fan

Telegram:

Most stupid coach I've seen. Had Notre Dame beaten in first quarter. Why 30 consecutive line plunges?

Gary, Ind.

A letter from a disappointed mother:

Dear Coach Rodgers,

I was looking forward to him being an all-American, not sitting on the bench. I would like to know as soon as possible (if he is going to play) as my husband is getting ready to come up there and pick him up. He says he'll just pay for him to go to another school . . .

A Football Mother

And from critics at large:

Dear Pepper,

I'll tell you one thing you long-haired clown; when the "Junkyard Dogs" (Georgia) get thru with your wishbone, there won't be enough meat left to make a bowl of soup at the Mission . . .

Rodgers Hater

Rodgers—

What will fill the stands at Tech is a new sensible coach. The average Tech fan doesn't like that kind of crap. Win yes, but with dignity. How can we stand Pepper for three more years?

Old Guard

Then there is the letter from a Kansas starter to a highly influential alumnus:

Dear Mr. ——:

How is everything going? Fine I hope. Thanks for getting me the job during the spring break. Is there any way possible you can loan me $50.00 to take care of my bills?

Thank you,

Kansas Starter

And the return letter:

Dear Kansas Starter:

The way you played in the Missouri game, I should have 50 coming from you.

Sincerely

Kansas Alumnus

And the high-brow advice to a football coach:

Dear Coach Rodgers,
When I watch you coach, I know the kind of coach I would like to have had. After seeing those onsides kick plays, a play popped into my mind. I don't know its feasability with your particular game, but it's just an idea. To make field goals easier, getting and setting the ball in the center of the field would result from this play.

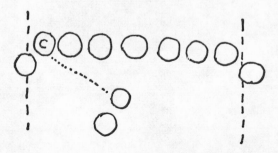

The center of course would be cockeyed but he is still there to block outside. A little pizzazz!

Pegasus

And, finally, the real ugly letter:

All Pepper Rodgers talks about is niggers.
And I am not a racist.

                                        Unsigned

As shown in this chapter, a lot goes on behind the scenes in college football, from hate mail from little kids, to all kind of advice, all free, to praise when you're winning and unholy Hades when we're losing. But it is all part of the great game of football, and I accept it all, the criticism along with the compliments. But I do appreciate logic.

Chapter XII   All Roads Lead Back to
Peachtree Street

Pepper Rodgers has three credos, (1) keep it simple on the field, (2) keep it changing off the field, and (3) keep them entertained and laughing on television. He is adept at all three. His Georgia Tech team runs the wishbone offenses with no frills; he calls it the "vanilla" or pure wishbone. In his off-field life he pitches changeups every day, never falling into a predictability pattern. Just when you think you have him figured out, you are in another ball park and the process starts over again. His television show is the hit of local programing in Atlanta, and it is his pride and joy. It is directed not at the football fan, but at the general audience, women, children, scholars, hard hats.

He operates on the variety show format in that he feeds celebrities to the public in wholesale lots. Entertainers playing in town call him and ask for the exposure. He has no trouble finding a Sunday cast. In the past two years "The Pepper Rodgers Show," a half-hour quick-moving program that includes a minimum of football, has offered such names as Burt Reynolds, Gregg Allman, Jack Cassidy, Mike Connors, Norm Crosby, Ed Nelson, David Brenner, Bob Hope, Al Hirt, Ronald Reagan, Edie Adams, Jimmy Carter, Kaye Stephens, George Kirby, Julia Childs, and Evel Knievel.

"You're a legend in your time," said Burt Reynolds, using his own script. "Pepper, as a player, you could not run, your passes looked like dead ducks, and you had funny knees and a bad face. As a former Florida State football player, I have one request. Give them a break. Lose to Florida State."

"Why don't you play more Jewish kids?" asked David Brenner on the program.

"Why don't you pass more?" asked Ronald Reagan.

For the odd-ball stunt of all time, Julia Childs cooked on the show. Can you imagine an unshaven football fan, brew in hand, watching Julia Childs cook? Or Woody Hayes announcing that for this recipe she uses two eggs and a dash of cinnamon?

Having spent considerable time in Los Angeles and Hollywood in the company of show business people—vis-à-vis, tennising with Chad Everett, Dale Robertson, Michael Landon, Dinah Shore, Charlton Heston, Doug McClure, George Peppard, Rod Steiger and golfing with Bill Russell, Keith Erickson, and Jerry West—Rodgers is sophisticated in the ways of gaining and holding the interest of audiences. His formula is to gain their attention at the start, not with a two-by-four as in the case of the old mule, but by something different. He opened one program by singing "I'm a rambling wreck from Georgia

Tech" . . . standing on his head. On another he had Oscar Fobbs, long-time football porter, whistle "Ramblin' Wreck" and that was the highlight of Fobbs's career.

Rodgers' television shows and his general comportment in Atlanta must be taken in context. He is in competition with the professional football Falcons, baseball Braves, basketball Hawks, and hockey Flames, not to mention the at-large entertainment dollar.

In his twenty-two years at Georgia Tech, Bobby Dodd compiled a record of 165 victories, 64 losses, and 8 ties. In the seven-year interim from Dodd to Rodgers, the Yellow Jackets were 39-37-1. From the full houses of the 1950s and 1960s, when the only way to gain admission to a Tech game was to be born into inheritance or watch the obituary column and apply upon the death of an old ticket holder, attendance dwindled appreciably. A major reason was the invasion of Atlanta by the professional teams and their campaigns for the entertainment money. Strangely enough, Dodd blames the Braves more than the football rivals, the Falcons, "because they are in the sports news from February to October."

As usual, however, Rodgers' timing was good. He returned to Atlanta when the professional teams were habitual losers and the field wide open in the bidding for the Peachtree Street sports kingdom.

"Pepper is exactly what Georgia Tech needed," says Dodd, now retired as athletic director. "He is colorful, highly quotable, and a worthy adversary for the professionals."

There is no question of Rodgers' competitive nature.

Highly successful North Carolina basketball coach Dean Smith, an assistant at the Air Force Academy when Rodgers was on the football staff there, remembers Pepper as one who refused to concede.

"Pepper was proud of his tennis and he challenged our head basketball coach, Bob Spears, to a match," recalls Smith. "Now Spears was an outstanding player and we predicted he'd beat Pepper a love set, 6–0. This made Pepper indignant. 'It'd take Jack Kramer to beat me, 6–0,' he said.

"Well, Spears did in fact beat him, 6–0. To show you how competitive Pepper was, right after the set he said, 'Let's play another one, right now.' He didn't want to walk off that court a love-set loser.

"Every day thereafter he badgered Spears to play him again. And we had a lot of fun everytime we saw Pepper. We'd tease him with, 'Hey, Pepper, we just saw Jack Kramer coaching basketball.'"

Because of his single-minded competitiveness, Rodgers keeps the professionals on their toes. There is no match for his television show. While the Falcons have a half-hour program reciting such banalities as players' hobbies and the number of children they have and how they play a sideline pass and cautiously steering away from the "meat" of what people want to know about football, Rodgers takes the viewers into his half-time locker room and accepts criticism from the stands and answers penetrating questions. In this respect, he is far more professional than the professionals.

His show has an exceptionally high Nielson rating of 11. No other football show in the area has more than a 2.

His show draws rave reviews from critics throughout the country.

Don't be surprised if one of these days Rodgers has the President of the United States on his program.

In January of '76 a story broke out of Detroit that Judge Willis Ward, a black, had been a member of the University of Michigan team that played Georgia Tech in 1934 at Ann Arbor. Because of the objections of Southerners at that time, he was withheld from the game on the agreement that Tech would withhold its own starting end Hoot Gibson. The Michigan center for that game, one Gerald Ford, was so upset at the injustice of it all he almost quit the team, as the story goes.

The story made interesting reading. Later that afternoon a reporter visited Rodgers in his office and mentioned the Ward article.

"Oh, yes, that reminds me," he said as he dashed to the door and called to his secretary, Suzanne Blakeney.

"Suzanne, did President Ford call back?"

"No."

"Get him on the phone."

"Yes, sir."

Needless to say, Suzanne did not get President Ford on the line. This is not to say Pepper was not serious. He was. He fully expected Ford to pop on the line and say, "Hi, Pepper." That is Rodgers brashness. But then if he had not spoken up for himself when he wore a red shirt in

1951, he never would have been elevated to the varsity. He did not advance his coaching career by being a shrinking violet.

His long-time friend Doug Weaver knows about Rodgers and telephones.

"He is a compulsive phone caller," says Weaver.

There was a morning in 1967 when Weaver, then a law student at Kansas and an aide on the football team, missed the team plane to Lincoln for a game with Nebraska because of a law exam. He was to leave on a Saturday morning.

Before he could get out of his home and to the airport, the phone rang.

"What's happening?" asked the staccato voice from Lincoln.

"Heck, why did you call?" said Weaver. "I'm going to see you in two hours."

But he knows why Pepper called. He was there in the room and the phone was there. No use wasting a telephone.

As the Rodgers personality emerges from people who know him, it falls into two categories. Off the field he is totally uninhibited, but not unprogramed; on the field, he is all business and discipline.

"A lot of people misunderstand Pepper," says Weaver. "Sure he does a lot of goofy things, things he enjoys, but at the same time he is one of the finest technique coaches in the business. His strengths are fundamentals and offensive simplicity, seemingly contradictory to the unorthodox behavior off the field and on television, but those are two separate areas and he divides them in his mind.

"His charm lies in his inconsistency. What I am telling you might not be what he tells you. Consistency is not one of his virtues; inconsistency is what makes him fascinating. He is a keen, intuitive person, and what he did yesterday might not be what to do today. He has unreal timing."

At Kansas before the Missouri game of '67, Rodgers led his team on the field by doing a forward roll, not a somersault or a cartwheel, as some described it. He tucked his hands, grabbed his shins and came up on the ball of his feet, a gymnastic exercise. This unconventional behavior by a coach from an aloof and dignified profession was duly reported by the media. If there is anything coaches detest more than misbehavior of players, it is one of their own deviating from the norm. Coaches are so insecure as a group that they run the same plays and use the same defenses for fear of failing out in the open and being held to ridicule. It has been said a coach could dust off the old single-wing and confuse all the others, but that would never happen because he would be laughed out of town if he did not win.

Rodgers' acts are impromptu only in regard to timing. Before he did his forward roll, he practiced it, perhaps in his basement. He did not do it unprepared. He does not do anything unprepared. What it was, was practiced free expression. In other words, he uses a lot of the Bobby Riggs psychology. Riggs will practice dribbling a basketball up the stairs, then sit around and act like the thought just occurred to him and challenge someone to a contest of dribbling up the stairs.

"That's Pepper," says Weaver. "He knows exactly what he is doing. Most of the time when he appears to be shooting from the hip, it is all thought out. This is not to say he doesn't do things off the top of his head. He does. Even then, with his quick mind, they come out logically."

The inconsistency keeps people guessing and that is part of the Rodgers mystique. He can be a sound fundamentalist and the biggest put-on in the country at the same time. Those who are lulled by his off-field comportment are surprised by the soundness of his team. Watch the swinging medallion and you can lose the game.

Weaver says there is a reason why he is easily bored and needs spice in his life.

"He can do in three or four hours what it takes most people all day to do," he says. "Not that he is fast. He is more productive.

"He has a lot of spare time and he fills most of it reading everything he can get his hands on, newspapers, magazines, wallpaper, shirt labels, anything."

Tommy Prothro, Rodgers' mentor at UCLA who moved from there to the Los Angeles Rams and then to the San Diego Chargers, agrees on the assessment.

"Pepper's image as a razzle-dazzle coach was something concocted by newspapermen," he says. "In reality he is a sound fundamentalist and a great teacher. He brought to UCLA a refreshing and different outlook, and we changed our style because of him. His football philosophy was probably misinterpreted because he can describe an off-tackle play and make it sound like a triple reverse."

Prothro's words are reinforced by the Rodgers who returned to Georgia Tech, not with a sleeper play, or a statue of liberty, or unbridled passing, but with power football off the wishbone formation and featuring such running talent as David Sims, Adrian Rucker, Pat Moriarity, Eddie Lee Ivery, and Tony Head behind a strong and aggressive offensive line. He took a defensive back, Danny Myers, and made a consistent quarterback out of him. Myers' backup, Rudy Allen, was the superior passer, but he could also run, a prerequisite for the wishbone.

To the critics who say he should pass more, Rodgers has an answer.

"Show me a predominantly passing team and I'll show you a loser," he says. "People say the wishbone is not a big-play offense, and I say how many runners averaged more than Sims' eight yards per carry? At UCLA in 1973 we led the nation in rushing, and at Georgia Tech in 1975 we were third."

In Frank Sinatra's sentiments, Pepper Rodgers goes on doing things his way.

"He's his own man," says Red McDaniel, who played tackle for him at Georgia Tech. "He demands perfection on the field, but he treats everybody with respect and he doesn't try to direct what you do off the field. He's your coach. He doesn't also try to be your daddy. He figures his players have to grow up, and he lets them do it."

When Georgia beat Tech, 42–26, in 1975 after losing,

34–14, during Rodgers' first year, Bulldog offensive lineman Randy Johnson said the victory was sweet over "a
coach who talks too much."

"He is calling me a 'bigmouth' and you know what old
'bigmouth' is telling his players after the game?" says
Rodgers. "I am telling my players to treat other players
with respect and give them the proper credit for winning.
Now, if you ask me what my religion is, it is treat others
as you would like them to treat you."

Later Rodgers wrote a letter to Johnson congratulating
him on an all-America career.

With the dawning of 1976, Rodgers appeared more at
ease with himself. No longer was he the knight on the
white charger seeking to conquer greener pastures. Marriage to Janice and a return home had had a settling
influence on him.

"In those earlier days, going from the Air Force Academy to Florida, then to UCLA and Kansas, back to
UCLA and so on brought a new excitement into my life,"
he said. "Now I don't need that anymore. I am comfortable with myself. I like what I am, and I wonder how
many people can say that."

There were other changes, some sorrowful, some
happy.

In March of '76 the ancient, battered desk of the
"Downstairs Coach" in the Georgia Tech Athletic Department was vacated when Pepper's father, Franklin Cullen
Rodgers, Sr., died at the age of sixty-seven, bringing to an
end a warm and sentimental relationship that spanned a
lifetime. Franklin never strayed far from Pepper's side,

and upon his son's return to Georgia Tech he appointed himself as the unsalaried "Downstairs Coach," helping with recruiting, serving as a self-appointed employment agency for players, wives, and secretaries in the athletic department, and being the general handyman in the service of his son.

When Pepper ordered a soft drink machine, it ended up in the office of the "Downstairs Coach."

"Sometimes," Pepper said with a smile, "Franklin forgets who the head coach is."

In his own right, Franklin Rodgers was a legend around Atlanta. He was a regular at City Hall, mingling with politicians and running for offices for twenty years and landing only one—that on the Board of Education. For years he could be seen on Forsyth Street holding court with Pat Patterson, the Union Depot policeman, and often conspiring with Patterson to feed bourbon-soaked bread to pigeons.

"If he had been born of middle-class parents instead of being one of fourteen children in a depression family, he'd have been one of the most successful guys around," Pepper says. "He was aggressive and he had guts. He got thrown out of the seventh grade for throwing a T-square at Mr. Highdecker, the principal."

It was perhaps significant that Franklin Rodgers weakened and died when Pepper had made it big in his home town. He had spent a lifetime serving as a parental press agent for his son in Atlanta. "I had to keep his name before the public even if I had to tell a few white lies," Franklin Rodgers said a month before his death.

In his zeal, he had put Pepper on probation at Kansas University when he signed three players before the legal deadline. Then, after Big Eight commissioner Wayne Duke forbade Franklin to speak to prospects for a year, he skirted the dictum by relaying messages through his wife, Louise.

In all of his recruiting, he missed out on only one blue-chip player, and he told the story several months before his death.

He was after Joe Colquitt and he promised to wait until a Wednesday night when Colquitt's father would be home from work for the signing ceremony.

"Lo and behold, on Wednesday morning when I called Joe, he told me he had already signed with Kansas," Franklin Rodgers said. "He said a man appeared at his home at 1 A.M. Wednesday morning, said I couldn't make it, and Joe would have to sign at that time. I asked him to check the name on the contract. He was gone a few minutes and then returned. The name, he said, was 'Vince Gibson.'

"I had been snookered by our old rival from Kansas State. Ole Vince had beaten us to the punch. But I'm proud that Colquitt made the all-America teams, even if he did end up at Kansas State. It showed I knew what I was doing."

Later, when Gibson had moved over to coach at Louisville, one of his scouts returned with the news that "an old man was there making me feel like a fool and making a big play for the prospect."

Gibson smiled wryly. "That wasn't an ordinary old man. Damned if you didn't run into the master," he said.

Franklin was always ready to help a prospect. In 1975 when the coaches brought in a new signee, he burst into the office and offered to find the young man a job.

"What kind of job?" asked the player.

"Oh," said Franklin, "I know the foreman at the Hardin Construction Company."

Son Pepper almost fell out of his chair laughing.

"Franklin," he said, "I want you to meet Bo Hardin, whose family owns the Hardin Construction Company."

Franklin Rodgers signed a few players that Georgia Tech didn't even want. He explained that he acquired their signatures on grants-in-aid with the understanding he would take them to Pepper and try to sell him on approving "the loan," as in a used car sale. Naturally, the grants weren't legal because Pepper's name wasn't on them.

His explanation for the signings: "I was afraid some other school might get them."

There was no one quite like Franklin Rodgers, the "Downstairs Coach," a most unforgettable character, perhaps the last of a breed.

Pepper Rodgers once said that next to his father his closest friend and confidante was Doug Weaver, his assistant coach at Kansas and UCLA, and perhaps it was fate that soon after Franklin's death Weaver, upon the recommendation of Pepper, was named athletic director at Georgia Tech to succeed Bobby Dodd, who retired on June 30, 1976.

Once more Rodgers and Weaver, the "Odd Couple" from Los Angeles days, were reunited, this time, however, with Weaver as Rodgers' boss, technically, with rights to choose his own stations on his car radio.

When Rodgers left Kansas to go to UCLA as head coach, he took three assistants with him, Weaver, Terry Donahue, and Dick Tomey. Success smiled on these three of the old Kansas gang. While Rodgers and Weaver were teaming once more at Georgia Tech, Donahue, at age thirty-one, was named the head coach at UCLA to succeed Dick Vermeil, who moved on to the Philadelphia Eagles of the National Football League.

Football coaching is one big chess game.

As Rodgers says, he could have been a dancer, a singer, or an entertainer. Instead he chose to be a football coach.

"How can you beat it?" he says. "I haven't worked a day in my life. I've been on a forty-five-year holiday."

RANDALL LIBRARY-UNCW

3 0490 0444367 1